MW01222866

A Season In Words
A Coach's Guide to Motivation from the Preseason to the Postseason

Dan Spainhour

Educational Coaching & Business Communications, Winston-Salem, NC
www.ecbcommunications.com

A Season In Words
A Coach's Guide to Motivation from the Preseason to the Postseason

By: Dan Spainhour

ISBN 978-0-6151-7280-4

Educational Coaching & Business Communications
240 Valencia Circle
Winston-Salem, NC 27106

About the Author

Dan Spainhour has more than 20 years of high school and college coaching experience. He has received numerous awards during his accomplished career, including 14 coach of the year honors, and was named an ambassador for athletics in the state of North Carolina. His teams have collected more than 400 victories and three state championships. He received a master's degree in in sports administration from the University of Miami (Fla.), where he worked as part of the men's basketball staff. While at Miami, he helped lead the Hurricanes to their first NCAA tournament appearance in 38 years. Spainhour recently returned to high school coaching after serving as the director of basketball operations at Florida State University. During his time in Tallahassee, the Seminoles made the NIT Tournament. He is also the founder of East Coast Basketball Camps and is considered one of the country's leading teachers of basketball fundamentals, having instructed for Coach Mike Krzyzewski's camps at Duke University for 10 years, as well as camps for other top coaches across the country. He is the author of three books: *A Season In Words,* a motivational guide that leads coaches from the preseason to the postseason; *How To Get Your Child An Athletic Scholarship,* a leading instructional guide on recruiting and *How To Run A Basketball Camp,* a guide to directing a successful basketball camp.

Spainhour and his wife, Cara, live in Winston-Salem, North Carolina.

Contents

Introduction

I quote others to better express myself
—Montaigne

Like most coaches I really like quotes. I think they can be a powerful motivational tool for players. *A Season In Words* is my attempt to take you through your season and provide you with motivational quotes for situations as they arise. There are hundreds of thousands of quote books and many are targeted to coaches. However, they are not organized as the season is organized.

A Brief History

A number of years ago I began to collect quotes. I bought quote books—I especially like the little pocket-sized ones. Coaching friends often sent quotes to me and at every clinic or camp I attended, I seemed to come away with new quotations. Every time I would read an interesting passage or hear one cited I would jot it down or in some cases try to commit it to memory. After a few years my vast collection was completely unorganized. I found that whenever I needed a quote for a particular situation in the season, I wasted so much time searching for just the right one. All the books I had categorized quotes by subject but subject matter is not what I needed—I wanted seasonal matter. I mean DESIRE after a loss is different than DESIRE after a win. So one summer I decided to go through my quote collection and organize them as I would a season. I thought of things that normally occur within a season and I placed what I thought to be appropriate quotes in corresponding files. Each section of this publication represents one of my files.

What I've used for certain events you may find more appropriate for other times. I encourage you to use them as they best fit the needs of you and your team. Just because I have quotes cited in the preseason doesn't mean they would not be successful motivators for other parts of the season. As a matter of fact, many of the quotations that I liked the most were placed into several files and used at different times throughout the year. For the purpose of putting together this manual, I didn't think you would appreciate the same quote used throughout. So I encourage you to mix and match, move and choose as you see fit.

A Word About the Quotes

This is a collection of quotes that I have gathered throughout my 20 years of coaching. Some read, some given, some heard and possibly some even made up. As you will notice some are cited and some are not. One thing I've found about cited quotes is that they are often attributed to someone who only repeats what they've already heard. The purpose of this collection is not to assign proper credit, rather it is to provide a motivational tool for you. So if a player asks you who said a particular quote, feel free to respond as I have many times—***It's the message son—not the messenger that's important***.

File One

The Preseason

It has been said that teams are made during the season and players are made in the off-season. I have never liked the word off-season because it tends to send a message that when you are not in season you're off. I have always preferred to call anytime out of season as the preseason. Sure, I encouraged my players to get away from the game and to play other sports. But I wanted them to think of anytime out of season as a preparation for the following year. The following quotes are to help ensure that your athletes get the most out of their "preseasons".

If I had eight hours to chop down a tree, I'd spend six sharpening my ax.
Abraham Lincoln

What lies behind you, what lies before you is of very little importance compared to what lies within you.

The image of a champion is someone who is bent over drenched in sweat to the point of exhaustion—when no one else is watching.

People don't plan to fail, they just fail to plan.

The first principle is that you must not fool yourself—and you are the easiest person to fool.

We lie loudest when we lie to ourselves.

History will be kind to me for I intend to write it.

Rule your mind or it will rule you.

You're never going to be driven anywhere worthwhile. But you sure as hell can drive yourself to a lot of great places.
Bob Knight

Maybe it wasn't the talent the Lord gave me—maybe it was the passion.
Wayne Gretsky

If I had only done today what I set out for yesterday I'd be free tomorrow.
Wayne Dyer

It wasn't raining when Noah built the ark.

I don't believe that God put us on this earth to be ordinary.
Lou Holtz

The shortest distance between two points is usually under repair.

You need to decide whether you want a life of comfort or a life of accomplishment.

The Preseason

Lazy people are always looking for something to do.

Always set goals but never set limits.

There is no such thing as great talent without great willpower.

The world is filled with willing people, some willing to work, some willing to let them work.

Twenty years from now you will be more disappointed by the things that you didn't do than by the ones you did. So throw off the bowlines. Sail away from the safe harbor. Catch the trade winds in your sails. Explore. Dream. Discover.
Mark Twain

It's never crowded along the extra mile.

One discipline always leads to another discipline.

I've learned that if you have a chance you better take it. Life is too precious. I always tell my players to enjoy the now.
Gary Williams

The time is always right to do what is right.
Martin Luther King Jr.

What people say, what people do, and what they say they do are entirely different things.

Our minds are lazier than our bodies.

Footprints on the sands of time are not made by sitting down.

Discipline is the bridge between goals and accomplishments.

It is one of the strange ironies of this strange life that those who work the hardest, who subject themselves to the strictest discipline, who give up certain pleasurable things in order to achieve a goal, are the happiest men. When you see 20 or 30 men line up for a distance race in some meet, don't pity them, don't feel sorry for them. Better envy them instead.

First we form habits, then they form us. Conquer your bad habits or they will conquer you.

In reading the lives of great men, I found that the first victory they won was over themselves—self-discipline with all of them came first.
Harry S. Truman

The difference between an extraordinary player and an ordinary player is that little extra.

Work is good. For too many people work has a negative connotation. They're the excuse makers. Workers are winners.

Extra discipline makes up for a lack of talent and a lack of discipline quickly siphons away extra talent, that's why it's frequently the most disciplined rather than the most gifted who rise to the top.

If you want your dreams to come true, get out of bed.

Imagination is more important than knowledge.

Those who have invested the most are the last to surrender.

Act the way you'd like to be and soon you'll be the way you act.

When it comes to getting things done, we need fewer architects and more bricklayers.

I know the price of success: dedication, hard work, and an unremitting devotion to the things you want to see happen.
Frank Lloyd Wright

Don't waste life in doubts and fears; spend yourself on the work before you, well assured that the right performance of this hour's duties will be the best preparation for the hours and ages that will follow it.
Ralph Waldo Emerson

Opportunity is missed by most because it is dressed in overalls and looks like work.
Thomas J. Edison

Success of the striver eliminates the pain of the striving.

To be on the top you must first get off your bottom.

It's choice not chance that determines your destiny.

The most important thing in a person's life is his faith and how he translates his faith into practical deeds.
Hakeem Olajuwon

What you are as a person is far more important that what you are as a player.
John Wooden

R.E.P.S.- Repetition Elevates Personal Skills.

The person who does what he pleases is seldom pleased with what he does.

Followers will never get any farther than their leaders.

The hardest thing about climbing the ladder of success is getting through the crowd at the bottom.

Failure to prepare is preparing to fail.

The best preparation for tomorrow is doing your best today.

Before everything else, getting ready is the secret to success.

The time to repair the roof is when the sun is shining.

John F. Kennedy

Talent alone won't make you a success. Neither will being in the right place at the right time, unless you are ready. The most important question is: Are you ready?

Johnny Carson

Unless a man has trained himself for his chance, the chance will only make him look ridiculous.

Success depends upon previous preparation, and without such preparation there is sure to be failure.

If it is worth playing, it is worth paying the price to win.

Bear Bryant

The most prepared are the most dedicated.

The best preparation for good work tomorrow is to do good work today.

The secret of happiness is not in doing what one likes, but liking what one does.

Things may come to those who wait, but only those things left by those who hustle.

Abraham Lincoln

Hold yourself responsible for a higher standard than anybody else expects of you. Never excuse yourself.

Henry Ward Beecher

Genius is 1 percent inspiration and 99 percent perspiration.

The difference between a successful person and others is not a lack of strength, nor a lack of knowledge but rather a lack of will and desire.

Vince Lombardi

The quality of a person's life is in direct proportion to their commitment to excellence, regardless of their chosen field of endeavor.
Vince Lombardi

It is our decisions and not the conditions that determine our destiny.

If you aren't going all the way, why go at all?

The best kink of pride is that which compels a man to do his very best work, even if no one is watching.

Goals are dreams with a time limit.

We are a product of the choices we make, not the circumstances that we face.

If you want something bad enough; then no matter how bad it gets you'll get it.

The key to willpower is wantpower. People who want something bad enough can usually find the willpower to achieve it.

Even the longest journey begins with a single step.

Never give up on a dream just because of the time it will take to accomplish it. The time will pass anyway.

The only easy day was yesterday.

Your toughest competition in life is anyone who is willing to work harder than you.

Today's preparation determines tomorrow's achievement.

The secret in life is to be ready for your opportunity when it comes.

No one ever attains true success by simply doing what is required of him; it's the amount of effort over and above the required that determines ultimate greatness.

Don't let dreaming get in the way of doing.

Everybody wants to win championships once the season starts. The key is to want to win them in the off-season.

Everybody wants to go to heaven, but nobody wants to die.

What you plant now, you will harvest later.

For the unwavering and determined there is time and opportunity.

There will come a time when the winter will ask what you were doing all summer.

The game of life is like the game of boomerangs. Our thoughts, deeds and words return to us sooner or later with astounding accuracy.

You will maximize your potential when you are willing to give up at any moment all that you are to receive all that you can become.

If at first you DO succeed, try something harder.

It's the start that stops most people.

We use to practice in the gym at the high school; then, on the way home, we'd stop and play on the playgrounds until eight o'clock. I played when I was cold and my body was aching and I was so tired...and I don't know why, I just kept playing and playing and playing.
Larry Bird

If the word quit is part of your vocabulary, then the word finish is likely not.

Great minds have purpose, others have wishes.

Your thoughts become your words. Your words become your actions. Your actions become your habits. Your habits become your character. Your character becomes your destiny.

Good, better, best. Never let it rest. Until your good is better and your better is best.

You don't get to choose when opportunity is going to knock, so you better be prepared for it when it does.

It's so hard when you have to, but so easy when you want to.

Be careful that you don't choose the comforts of mediocrity over the toil of success.

It takes courage to push yourself to places you have never been before—to test your limits—to break through barriers.

A man's future is molded by his own hands.

Opportunity rarely knocks on your door. Instead knock on opportunity's door if you really wish to enter.

You will become as small as your controlling desire; or as great as your dominant aspiration.

Our aspirations are our possibilities.

We are told never to cross a bridge until we come to it, but this world is owned by people who have crossed bridges in their imagination far ahead of the crowd.

The indispensable first step to getting the things you want out of life is deciding exactly what it is you want.

Desire must come from within, not as a result of being driven by coaches and parents.

The more you discipline yourself, the less you'll be disciplined by others.

I learned that if you want to make it bad enough, no matter how bad it is, you can make it.

Gale Sayers

Winning starts with beginning.

An athlete with no ambition is an athlete in poor condition. That applies in both the mental and physical sense. There is no substitute for desire. It can make a mediocre athlete into a good one and a good athlete into a great one.

If you want to be successful, do the things successful people do.

The man on the top of the mountain didn't just fall up there.

Faith is to believe what you do not yet see; the reason for faith is to see what you believe.

Ask yourself, what are you willing to do to make it the way you want it to be?

Half of getting what you want is knowing what you must give up to get what you want.

If you don't start something, it's certain you won't finish it.

Players are made in the off-season, teams are made during the season.

It's not the push from behind, or the pull from up front, but rather the drive from within.

Don't wallow in the mud with pigs, you will get dirty....and the pigs will like it.

Nothing will work unless you do.
John Wooden

The only place that success is before work is in the dictionary.

I learned early that if I wanted to achieve anything in life, I'd have to do it myself. I learned that I had to be accountable.
Lenny Wilkens

It's not the hours you put in, it's what you put in the hours.

Be more concerned with your character than your reputation.
John Wooden

There are two pains in life, the pain of discipline, and the pain of regret. Take your choice.

Remember this, the choices you make in life, make you.
John Wooden

In life you are given two ends, one to think with the other to sit on. Your success in life depends on which end you use the most.

Be at the right place, at the right time, and do the right thing.

He who floats with the current, who does not guide himself according to higher principles, who has no ideal, no real standards—such a man is a mere article of the world's furniture—a thing moved, instead of a living and moving being—an echo, not a voice.

Be a hard master to yourself and be lenient to everybody else.

We need people who influence their friends and who cannot be detoured from their principles by friends who do not have the courage to have any principles.
Joe Paterno

Don't quest for popularity at the expense of morality.

What is popular is not always right, and what is right is not always popular.
Daniel Webster

The higher your standards—the better you become at what you do.

You can fake out fans, coaches, and mom and dad, but you can't fake out yourself.

I care not what others think of what I do, but I care very much about what I think of what I do.

Theodore Roosevelt

The measure of a man's real character is what he would do if he knew he would never be found out.

Without the burn, you will never learn.

Everyone wants to win, but not everyone is willing to prepare to win.

Bob Knight

One day of practice is like one day of clean living. It doesn't do you any good.

It is easier to stay out than get out.

Mark Twain

What it lies in our power to do, it lies in our power not to do.

Aristotle

What we do upon some great occasion will probably depend on what we already are. What we are will be the result of previous years of self-discipline.

Stand by your convictions. If you say what you think, you're called cocky or conceited. But if you have an objective in life, you shouldn't be afraid to stand up and say it. In the second grade, they asked us what we wanted to be. I said I wanted to be a ballplayer and they laughed. In the eight grade, they asked the same questions and they laughed a little more. By the eleventh grade, no one was laughing.

Johnny Bench

The only discipline that lasts is self discipline.

Bum Phillips

Anybody who gets away with something will come back to get away with a little bit more.

A winner is someone who sets his goals, commits himself to these goals, and pursues these goals with all the ability given him.

It's not the work that's hard, it's the discipline.

You show me a boy or a girl with a desire to win and I'll show you a person who will work hard the thousands if hours it takes to win. Show me those who want to go to the top and I'll show you people who will take coaching. They will welcome it. They will beg for it. They will use every God-given talent they have to its utmost. They will drink in inspiration. If they lack desire, they won't work. They won't take coaching.

Bob Richards
Two-time Olympic Gold Medalist

The off-season is the time to improve and the season is the time to prove.

Our future will be a direct reflection of our work and improvement.

The first and the best victory is to conquer self.

Plato

Discipline is remembering what you want.

Discipline—possessing the inner strength to commit yourself to the rules, regulations and training needed to achieve excellence and sticking to them.

What we think or what we believe is, in the end, of little consequence. The only thing of consequence is what we do.

One day I had an epiphany. I said to myself yes I am different. But instead of that being a bad thing I can have the best of two worlds. I learned to love to be unique.

Shane Battier

We are what we repeatedly do. Excellence, then, is not an act, but a habit.

Aristotle

That government is best which governs the least, because its people discipline themselves.

Thomas Jefferson

File Two

The Beginning
& Practice
Quotes

The season starts, enthusiasm is high. The process begins. Tryouts. Early season practices are a time to set a tone for the upcoming season. No detail is too small. It is a time to encourage hard work, sacrifices, fundamentals, toughness and goals. The quotes in this section provide inspiration to get the most out of the start of the season and each and every practice that follows.

What we want to see is players in pursuit of knowledge, not knowledge in pursuit of players.

A pint of sweat will save a gallon of blood.

Building a team is like constructing a building. You start with solid footings and a strong foundation. Conditioning is the footing and fundamentals are the foundation.

Ability is what you're capable of doing, motivation determines what you do, attitude determines how well you do it.

No coach ever won a game by what he knows; it's what his players have learned.

Everything should be made as simple as possible, but not one bit simpler.

Eyes are more accurate witness then ears.

Education is learning what you didn't even know you didn't even know.

If the only thing you think about is the future, it's going to be somebody else's.

People want to see national championship banners. People want to talk about us being competitive. How do we get there? We don't get there with milk and cookies.
Bob Knight

Natural abilities are like natural plants—they need pruning by correct study.
Red Auerbach

The greatest mistake is to continue practicing a mistake.

Leadership is getting someone to do what they don't want to do to achieve what they want to achieve.
Tom Landry

It's the little things that make big things happen.

Never look where you're going look where you want to go.

The more you sweat in practice, the less you bleed in battle.

That which we persist in doing becomes easier for us to do; not that the nature of the thing itself has changed but our ability to do it has increased.

Ralph Waldo Emerson

Getting something done is an accomplishment; getting something done right is an achievement.

Know the true value of time; snatch, seize and enjoy every moment of it.

Once you get a camel's nose in a tent his body will soon follow.

It's okay to be a late bloomer. What's important is just that you bloom.

Success comes from a creation of desire not a creation of need.

To climb steep hills requires a slow pace at first.

Making long term commitments require short term difficulties.

It is not the need but the appetite that makes eating a delight.

There's a fine line between being conceited and having confidence in yourself. Conceited is thinking you can do it without the hard work and perseverance.

The starting point of all achievement is desire.

You must be willing to sacrifice all other things to accomplish a level of superiority.

A winner's strongest muscle is his heart.

Work is the meat of life, pleasure the dessert.

You are making progress if each mistake is a new one.

The difference between average teams and very good teams is that good teams do not surrender to fatigue.

Rick Pitino

A short time of discomfort is far better than a lifetime of regret.

I will get ready and then perhaps my chance will come.

Abraham Lincoln

All hard work brings a profit, but mere talk leads only to poverty.
Proverbs 14:23

Mistakes are stepping stones to success.

If you make a mistake do not alibi—learn why.

A professional is a man who can do his job when he doesn't feel like it. An amateur is a man who can't do his job when he does feel like.

Before you can be great, first you must be good. Before you can be good, you must be bad. Before you can be bad, first you must try.

The only people who don't make mistakes are the people doing nothing.

All things are difficult before they are easy.

A minute lost in practice is never found.

Sports teaches that you can make a mistake one minute, let it go and be brilliant the next.

Luck is what happens when preparation meets opportunity.

Good players can take coaching. Great players can take coaching and learn.
John Wooden

A winner makes commitments—a loser makes promises.

If you can conceive it and believe it you can achieve it.

The first and most important step toward success is the feeling that we can succeed.

Progress is impossible without change; and those who cannot change their minds cannot change anything.

If you cannot do great things; do small things in a great way.

We're not going to take votes. I'm going to give you a clear picture of where this boat is going. What I expect from you is to get on board and put your oars in the water and start rowing
Coach Randy Walker

Paying attention to simple little things that most men neglect makes a few men rich.

Do what you can, with what you have, where you are.

Enthusiasm is the greatest asset in the world. It beats money and power.

It takes less time to do a thing right than it does to explain why you did it wrong.

Every season is a journey. Every journey is a lifetime.

                    Mike Krzyzewski

It takes no talent to work hard.

It's easy to have faith in yourself and discipline when you're a winner. What you've got to have is faith and discipline when you are not yet a winner.

Do you really understand all of what you think you know?

The man who says it can't be done is usually interpreted by the person that is doing it.

You are successful the moment you start moving toward a worthwhile goal.

Learn to listen. Sometimes opportunity knocks very softly.

Killing time murders opportunities.

A major part of success lies in the ability to put first things first. The reason most goals are not achieved is that we spend our time doing second things first.

If you can't see where you're going, you may not like where you end up.

If there is no struggle, there is no progress.

Positive anything is better than negative nothing.

The game is survival of the fittest. The strong survive, the weak do not.

When you see a successful individual, a champion, you can be very sure that you are looking at an individual who pays great attention to the perfection of minor details.

There are no secrets to success; Don't waste time looking for them. Success is the result of perfection, hard work, learning from failure, loyalty to those for who you work and persistence.

                    Colin Powell

The desire of perfection is the worst disease that ever afflicted the human mind.

When you're through changing, you're through.

The only thing that really counts is "are we getting better each day?"

Never expect to see perfect from an imperfect man.

There can be no happiness if the things we believe in are different from the things we do.

Only the mediocre are always at their best.

Lou Holtz's 3 Laws of Success

1. Do what's right
2. Do the best you can
3. Treat others as you would like to be treated

All the greats know how to keep it simple.

The eye's a better pupil, much more willing than the ear.

The only thing that stands between a man and what he wants from life is often merely the will to try it and the faith to believe that it is possible.

Wise counsel is confusing but example is always clear.

All our dreams can come true if we have the courage to pursue them.
Walt Disney

Fundamentals become natural through repetition.

Habits are unconscious acts that were once conscious.

The only mistake that is inexcusable is the mistake made from a lack of effort.

Weak desires bring weak results, just as a small amount of fire makes a small amount of heat.

The quality of a person's life is in direct proportion to their commitment to excellence, regardless of their chosen field of endeavor.
Vince Lombardi

If there's a way to do it better...find it.
Thomas Edison

The greatest mistake a man can make is to be afraid of making one.

This one step—choosing a goal and sticking to it—changes everything.

People with goals succeed because they know where they're going.

If you don't know where you're going, how can you expect to get there?

The most important thing about a goal is having one.

A man without a purpose is like a ship without a rudder.

There is no right way to do something wrong.

Work joyfully and peacefully, knowing that right thoughts and right efforts will inevitably bring about right results.

To measure the man measure his heart.

In the middle of difficulty lies opportunity.

Albert Einstein

Successful people keep moving. They make mistakes but they don't quit.

Conrad Hilton

All great achievements require time.

Some people have thousands of reasons why they can't do something when all they need is one reason why they can.

Success requires responsibility.

Things will come your way once you understand that you have to make it come your way by your own exertions.

You can't steal second and keep your foot on first.

Do not wish to be anything but what you are and try to be that perfectly.

St. Francis De Sales

If a man is called to be a street sweeper, he should sweep streets even as Michelangelo painted or Beethoven composed music or Shakespeare wrote poetry. He should sweep streets so well that all the hosts of heaven and earth will pause to say, here lived a great street sweeper who did his job well.

Martin Luther King, Jr.

Many receive advice, only the wise profit from it.

You've got to be in position for luck to happen. Luck doesn't go around looking for a bum.

You've got to be very careful if you don't know where you are going, because you might not get there.
Yogi Berra

Every job is a self-portrait of the person who did it.

Most people use a mirror to look at their outside appearance. Successful people use it to look at their inside appearance.

It's what you learn after you know it all that counts.

If you don't invest very much then defeat doesn't hurt very much and winning is not very exciting.

The road to success is paved with good intentions.

Do not let what you cannot do interfere with what you can do.

We cannot direct the wind...but we can adjust the sails.

Don't do more than you can do, but don't do less either.

Knowledge is a process of piling up facts. Wisdom lies in their simplification.

In practice, if you don't like to do it, it is probably good for you.

The smaller the detail the greater the value.

What to do with a mistake—recognize it, admit it, learn from it, forget it.
Dean Smith

I hear and I forget, I see and I remember, I do and I understand.

Tired equals dumb.

If you've got nothing to do, don't do it here.

There is time enough for everything in the course of the day if you do but one thing at once; but there is not time enough in the year if you will do two things at a time.
Lord Chesterfield,
(1747, from Letters to His Son)

Mental is to physical, as four is to one.
Bob Knight

To be successful, you don't have to do extraordinary things. Just do ordinary things extraordinarily well.

Excellence is the unlimited ability to improve the quality of what you have to offer.

Rick Pitino

People wish to learn to swim and at the same time to keep one foot on the ground.

It does not matter how slowly you go as long as you do not stop.

Keep it simple, when you get too complex you forget the obvious.

Al Maguire

Effort is only effort when it begins to hurt.

A good garden may have some weeds.

One can define discipline as—Doing what you have to do, doing it as well as you possibly can and doing it that way all the time.

First master the fundamentals.

Larry Bird

Play with heart everyday and you become very difficult to scout.

Never compromise on what you know is right.

If I accept you as you are, I will make you worse; however; if I treat you as though you are what you are capable of becoming, I help you become that.

The greatest of all faults is to be conscious of none.

How desperately difficult it is to be honest with oneself. It is much easier to be honest with other people.

Sometimes it is more important to discover what one cannot do, than what one can do.

Everybody has limits. You just have to learn what your own limits are and deal with them accordingly.

All progress has resulted from people who took unpopular positions.

It is better to be hated for what you are than loved for what you are not.

Never tell a young person that something cannot be done. God may have been waiting for centuries for somebody ignorant enough of the impossible to do just that thing.

You must have long-range goals to keep you from being frustrated by short range failures.

Develop a love for details. They usually accompany success.

John Wooden

Only the person who has the persistence to do the small things perfectly will acquire the skills necessary to do the big things well.

You cannot consistently perform in a manner which is inconsistent with the way you see yourself.

Each one of you need to accept the fact that from this moment on the direction and future of this team is in capable hands—yours.

There is always a demand for dedicated and enthusiastic players.

You've got to believe deep inside yourself that you're destined to do great things.

We're not asking you to be any stronger or quicker. We're asking you to be as good as you are. That's all it takes.

Bob Knight

Mistakes are a fact of life. It's the response that counts.

You can rely on self-disciplined individuals.

Twelve Required Commitments of Program Players

To Stay in the Program:

1. Be Committed To Your Academics
2. Be Committed To Having Class
3. Be Committed To Doing The Right Thing
4. Be Committed To Reputation of The Program

To Play in the Program:

1. Be Committed To Hard Work
2. Be Committed To Becoming A Smart Player
3. Be Committed To Having A Team Attitude
4. Be Committed To Having A Winning Attitude

To Win in the Program:

1. Be Committed To Our Philosophy
2. Be Committed To Yourself (Confidence)
3. Be Committed To Your Teammates
4. Be Committed To Your Coaches

If Coach Parcells tells you there's cheese on the mountain, you'd better bring crackers.

Keith Byars

Never confuse motion with action.
Benjamin Franklin

Change is a challenge to the adventurous and opportunity to the alert and a threat to the insecure.

Shallow men believe in luck, believe in circumstances: it was somebody's name, or he happened to be at the right place at the right time, or it was so then and another day it would have been different. Strong men believe in cause and effect.
Ralph Waldo Emerson

If you do not pay attention to the details of the game, you can believe your players never will.

Don't mistake activity with achievement.

Practice does not make perfect. Practice makes permanent.

Practice does not make perfect. Perfect practice makes perfect.

Pain is temporary; pride is forever.

A few months sacrifice; a lifetime of memories.

Cab drivers are living proof that practice does not make perfect.
Howard Ogden

Not doing more than the average is what keeps the average down.

The average person puts only 25 percent of his energy and ability into his work. The world takes off its hat to those who put in more than 50 percent of their capacity, and stands on its head for those few and far between souls who devote 100 percent.
Andrew Carnegie

Man can believe the impossible, but can never believe the improbable.
Oscar Wilde

In creating, the only hard thing is to begin—a grass blade is no easier to make than an oak.

Half this game is ninety percent mental.
Yogi Berra

To be conscious that you are ignorant is a great step to knowledge.

Learning without thought is labor lost; thought without learning is perilous.

That is what learning is. You suddenly understand something you've understood all your life, but in a new way.

Much learning does not teach understanding.

Whenever you are asked if you can do a job, tell 'em, 'Certainly I can!' Then get busy and find out how to do it.

Theodore Roosevelt

Learning is not compulsory—neither is survival.

There are people who, instead of listening to what is being said to them, are already listening to what they are going to say themselves.

Be a good listener. Your ears will never get you in trouble.

A player is only as good as his fundamentals and a team is only as good as its execution of both individual and team fundamentals.

Know how to listen, and you will profit even from those who talk badly.

Whenever I hear, 'It can't be done,' I know I'm close to success.

Success is not the result of spontaneous combustion. You must set yourself on fire.

A minute's success pays the failure of years.

In theory there is no difference between theory and practice. In practice there is.

Yogi Berra

It is a rough road that leads to the heights of greatness.

To give yourself the best possible chance of playing to your potential, you must prepare for every eventuality. That means practice.

Habits are cobwebs at first; cables at last.

File Three

Team Formation

One of the most important goals of any team sport is the formation of the team. Few things are as beautiful as a group of individuals that give up selfish desires and act as one unit. All successful teams have good leaders and players who accept their roles. Getting everyone on the same page is one of the coach's biggest challenges, especially in a society that often preaches a me-first attitude. A coach is wise if he does a little something everyday to help develop team chemistry. Here are a few quotes that may help.

If a house is divided against itself, that house cannot stand.

Try to be like him who will be like you.

Commitment is like ham and eggs. The chicken makes a contribution but the pig makes a commitment.

If I cannot do great things then I can do small things in a great way.

A team is a fist—not five fingers.
                                  Mike Krzyzewski

A star can win any game—a team can win every game.

The strength of a team is each individual member. The strength of each member is the team.
                                  Phil Jackson

Our goal is not to win. It's to play together and play hard. Then winning takes care of itself.
                                  Mike Krzyzewski

Some people believe you win with your five best players, but I found you win with the five who fit together best.
                                  Red Auerbach

It's how the team's average player performs that gives the team consistency and substance.

Whether it's in business, politics, education, or athletics, there has to be respect and loyalty for the leader. Success or failure depends on it. There are three questions from the leader that must be answered affirmatively by the group members if the group needs assurance that it can reach its desired goal. Can I trust you? Are you committed? Do you respect or care about me? If the individual can answer yes to their leader to these three questions, even greatness is within their grasp.
                                  Lou Holtz

You know you are a team player when:

- You realize fulfilling your role, whatever that role is, is most important

- You have a desire to excel for the benefit of those relying on you

- You have an unquenchable need to exceed your past limitations

- You play and know, without a doubt, that you competed like a champion

- You understand your commitment to your teammates

- You finish playing and only your body leaves the floor—your heart and soul are captured within the game

- You will exchange your blood, sweat, and tears for the benefit of the team

- You understand the irrelevance of individual awards

- You would rather encourage a teammate to success than benefit personally from his mistakes

- Your respect for the game outweighs your personal pride

- You make mistakes and use them to improve instead of using them as excuses

- Your ability to make your teammates better increases each time you play

- You do the little things right when nobody is watching

- You serve your teammates with unselfish motives

- You understand your role and strive to perform it better

- You have done all you can and still feel you haven't done enough

- You play with pain without creating a scene

- You give more than what is asked and take less than what is deserved

- Your effort is constant and your play is consistent regardless of the situation.

I feel more strongly about this than anything else in coaching. Anybody who lacks the discipline who does not want to be a part of the team, who doesn't want to meet the requirements has to go. It's that simple.

Bud Wilkinson

The most important thing I look for in a player is accountability. You have to be accountable for who you are. You can't blame things on someone else.

Lenny Wilkins

That which is not good for the beehive can't be good for the bees.

Concentrate on how you play—not how long you play.

The process of getting there. All the blood sweat and tears. All the lumps, bruises and breaks. When you do something together as a team there's nothing like it in the world.

Joe Gibbs

The surest way to failure is to consider oneself more cleaver than others.

Even Jesus had trouble with 12 guys.

No man is an island.

If we go backward; it's not one person's fault—it's everyone's. If we go forward, it's not one person's achievement—it's everyone's.

Giving is the highest level of living.

No man was ever honored for what he received. Honor has been the reward for what he gave

Calvin Coolidge

When everyone on our team believes that our own personal signature is on everything our team does—then we have a chance to be a great team. And not until we believe that every ball we play with has our team's name on it will we be proud of our performance.

In battle, the best troops are sometimes killed early. The people who pick up their rifles and take over win the battles. It's the same in all aspects of life, you have to be ready when your turn comes.

On a great team everybody does the dirty job.

A leader can't make excuses. There has to be quality in everything you do. Off the court, on the court, in the classroom.

Michael Jordan

You can take the best team and the worst team and line them up and you would find very little physical difference. You would find an emotional difference. The winning team has dedication. It will have a core group of players who set the standards.

We all want to be important in our jobs. However, the person who thinks I am the most important part of the team should remember this. Life is like a bucket of water. We are a part of the whole. But how big is the hole that is left when we take away a large cup of water? The hole suddenly fills up and...so life goes. The nature of life is that there is always someone who can and will take your place, when you think you are irreplaceable.

A leader is interested in finding the best way—not his own way.
John Wooden

Working together precedes winning together.

One measure of leadership is the caliber of people who choose to follow.

When all your strength is in union all your danger is in discord.

When I am playing basketball I'm playing to win—nothing else. It means I'm going to be an example to my teammates of what having a winning attitude is all about. It means I'll have an attitude of unselfishness that keeps me craving for more championships for my team, not glory for myself. It means I'll set an example at every practice by practicing harder and longer than anybody else. It means I'll think we and not me every time I step onto the court.
Magic Johnson

Doing nothing for others is the undoing of one's self.
Horace Mann

Players who are team leaders do the following:

- They do not isolate themselves from others.

- They make it easy for teammates to communicate with them.

- They follow the 24 hour rule. (If you have any kind of problem with a teammate don't let more than 24 hours go by without addressing it.)

- They give attention to potentially difficult relationships that may not involve them.

Don't worry about the flies on the elephant's butt when the butt is right in front of you.

The best teams have chemistry. They communicate with each other and they sacrifice personal glory for the common goal.

Snowflakes are one of natures most fragile things, but just look what they can do when they stick together.

The selfless player's main concern is winning and the selfish player's main concern is playing.

A team coming together is a beginning. A team staying together is progress. A team working together is success.

The strength of the pack is the wolf, and the strength of the wolf is the pack.

Above all you must contribute your whole self to the team, not just your athletic self.

Phil Jackson

A team asks of every individual a contribution and it is up to that individual to discover what it should be.

The speed of the leader determines the pace of the pack.

Adaptable people are:

- Teachable
- Emotionally Secure
- Creative
- Service Minded

John Maxwell

The time to make friends is before you need them.

What is right is more important than who is right.

John Wooden

The greatest need is the need to be needed.

Nothing will ever be attempted if all possible objections must first be overcome.

On a team you must have an attitude of gratitude.

The level of cooperation on any team increases as the level of trust increases.

A team is like a wheelbarrow—it stands still until someone pushes it.

Never discourage anyone who continually makes progress, no matter how slow.

It is foolish to expect a young man to follow your advice and to ignore your example.

Individual commitment to a group effort. That's what makes a team work.

A person doesn't really become whole until he becomes a part of something that's bigger than himself.

It's amazing what can be accomplished when no one cares who gets the credit.

You don't get harmony when everybody sings the same note.

Instill the discipline needed to always tell the truth.

You must have respect, which is part of love, for those under your supervision. Then they will do what you ask and more.

What you should do best is share your enthusiasm.

Don't point a finger—lend a hand.

A candle loses nothing by lighting another candle.

Have more than thou showest' speak less than thou knowest

When I'm getting ready to persuade a man, I spend one third of the time thinking about myself—what I'm going to say and two thirds of the time thinking about him and what he is going to say.
Abraham Lincoln

Leadership is a privilege and with privilege comes responsibility.

Anger is the only thing to put off till tomorrow.

Personality can open doors, but only character can keep them open.

Never deprive someone of hope; it might be all they have.

You cannot live a perfect day without doing something for someone who will never be able to repay you.
John Wooden

There are two ways of exerting one's strength: one is pushing down, the other is pulling up.

A Leader Checklist:

- A leader is always full of praise

- A leader learns to use the phrases, "thank you" and "please" on his way to the top

- A leader is always growing

- A leader is possessed with his dreams

- A leader launches forth before success is certain

- A leader is not afraid of confrontation

- A leader talks about his own mistakes before talking about someone else's

- A leader is a person of honesty & integrity

- A leader has a good name

- A leader makes others better

- A leader is quick to praise and encourage the smallest amount of improvement

- A leader is genuinely interest in others

- A leader looks for opportunities to find someone doing something right

- A leader takes others up with him

- A leaders responds to his own failures and acknowledges them before others have to discover and reveal them

- A leader never allows murmuring—from himself or others

- A leader is specific in what he expects

- A leader holds accountable those who work with him

- A leader does what is right rather than what is popular

- A leader is a servant

I'd rather see a sermon than hear one any day.

I'd rather one walk with me than merely show the way.

I may misunderstand you and the high advice you give. But there's no misunderstanding how you act and live.

Almost everyday in this job, there is a challenge of some sort to the team's unity. A person pulling apart, maybe a guy on the bench exerting his own challenge to the system whether he's stepping out of his role or having developed it too far or maybe the guy's just moody.
Phil Jackson

If you put a plant in a jar. It will grow to take the shape of the jar. Let it grow by itself and it may grow so 20 jars can't hold it.
Mike Krzyzewski

If he works for you, you work for him.

It is better to deserve honors and not have them than to have them and not deserve them.
Mark Twain

You cannot do wrong without suffering wrong.
Ralph Waldo Emerson

Rather fail with honor than succeed by fraud.

Working together works.

If you're too busy to help those around you succeed, you're too busy.

As a coach, I play not my eleven best, but my best eleven.
Knute Rockne

Either we're pulling together or we're pulling apart.

People support what they help create.

No one has ever washed their rental car.

You become successful by helping others become successful.

Praise loudly and blame softly.

What affects everyone can best be solved by everyone.

A person too busy to take care of his teammates is like a mechanic too busy to take care of his tools.

Doing nothing for others is the undoing of oneself.

To get the best out of people choose to think and believe the best about them.

Give all the credit away.

John Wooden

No matter what accomplishments you make, somebody helps you.

Asking for help is a strength, not a weakness.

Teamwork is working together—even when apart.

The best team doesn't win nearly as often as the team that gets along best.

A successful team beats with one heart.

No one can whistle a symphony.

We didn't all arrive in the same ship but we're all in the same boat.

It doesn't matter who gets the credit. If the job gets done, the credit will come.

There is no better exercise than reaching down and lifting people up.

None of us is as smart as all of us.

Team leadership impacts team performance.

The coach is the team, and the team is the coach. You reflect each other.

A team will out perform a group of individuals every time.

Never let an individual dominate a team.

Successful teams build on the strengths of individual members.

The achievements of an organization is the result of the combined effort of each individual.

Vince Lombardi

The speed of the leader determines the rate of the pack.

The price of greatness is responsibility.

Winston Churchill

A team requires that the standards of community prevail over selfish personal impulses.

What's best for the team is all I ever wanted to do.

Grant Hill

People seldom improve when they have no other model but themselves to copy after.

A coach's responsibility is getting all his players playing for the name on the front of the jersey, not the one on the back.

Attitudes are contagious...Is yours worth catching?

True eloquence consists in saying all that should be said, and that only.

Winning is about having the whole team on the same page.

It doesn't matter who scores the points, it's who can get the ball to the scorer.

Larry Bird

If we were supposed to talk more than we listen, we would have two mouths and one ear.

Mark Twain

Sometimes a player's greatest challenge is coming to grips with his role on the team.

Unity begins with you.

Great teamwork is the only way we create the breakthroughs that define our careers.

Pat Riley

Blame is the cowards way out.

A compromise is the art of dividing a cake in such a way that everyone believes he has the biggest piece.

There is no twilight zone of honest— a thing is right or it's wrong.

Have integrity, never deceive anybody, and have your word good. Never deviate from that.

Conrad Hilton

Loyalty means nothing unless you'll willing to practice self-sacrifice.

Loyalty up and down the line. That's one quality an organization must have to be successful.

You may order and rive an individual but you cannot make him respect you.

Respect is a virtue which goes far beyond the emotion of liking.

You cannot do a kindness too soon because you never know how soon it will be too late.
                    Ralph Waldo Emerson

There is nothing so rewarding as to make people realize they are worthwhile.

Three key factors of leaders

1. Great leaders possess the ability to see ability in others.
2. Great leaders have the ability to help others discover their ability.
3. Great leaders have the ability to help others develop their ability.

Tis not enough to help the feeble up, but support him after.
                              Shakespeare

People need responsibility. They resist assuming it, but they cannot get along without it.
                              John Steinbeck

Alone we can do so little; together we can do so much.
                              Helen Keller

Never look down on anybody unless you're helping them up.
                              Jesse Jackson

The true measure of an individual is how he treats a person who can do him absolutely no good.

It is not fair to ask of others what you are not willing to do yourself.
                              Eleanor Roosevelt

A true friend is someone who is there for you when he'd rather be anywhere else.

The truth of the matter is that you always know the right thing to do. The hardest part is doing it.
                              Norman Schwarzkopf

Teamwork is the ability to work together toward a common vision. The ability to direct individual accomplishments toward organizational objectives. It is the fuel that allows common people to attain uncommon results.
                              Andrew Carnegie

Many of us are more capable than some of us . . . but none of us is as capable as all of us.

The nice thing about teamwork is that you always have others on your side.

Individuals play the game, but teams beat the odds.

When he took time to help the man up the mountain, lo, he scaled it himself.

A group becomes a team when all members are sure enough of themselves and their contributions to praise the skill of others.

When a team outgrows individual performance and learns team confidence, excellence becomes a reality.

                    Joe Paterno

TEAM = Together Everyone Achieves More.

The whole is greater than the sum of the parts.

A job worth doing is worth doing together.

File Four

Before a Game

Apprehension, nervousness, doubt, confidence, excitement. All these characteristics are involved before a game. As the coach, you must make sure your players are ready every game. The words found here are designed to do just that.

In life. As in chess, forethought wins.

You cannot discover new oceans unless you have the courage to lose sight of the shore.

Avoid paralysis through analysis.

The man who makes no mistakes does not usually make anything.

Do what has to be done, when it has to be done, as well as it can be done, and do it that way all the time.

My mom gave me unconditional support and unfailing love. You can't get any better than that. That's why I've never been afraid to lose.
                              Wayne Gretsky

Keep calm by making sure you don't concentrate on anything you can't control.

It's more important to remove barriers that keep you out of the "zone" than to try to figure out how to get in the "zone".

Accept the challenges so that you may feel the exhilaration of victory.
                    General George Patton

Every play you are to one to wear the hat. You have to make it happen. You have to take responsibility for yourself and you have to take responsibility for your team.

If you don't have butterflies, it's because you think you have no chance.

We are always getting ready to live, but never living.

Resolve that whatever you do, you will bring the whole man to it; that you will fling the whole weight of your being into it.

Learning is never complete until it is applied.

There is a big difference between doing it almost right and doing it right. The outcome of games are more the result of mistakes than great plays.
                              Bob Knight

Thinking too much about how you're doing when you're doing it is disastrous.

Don't forget to swing hard, in case you hit the ball.

Efforts and courage are not enough without purpose and direction.

There is no future in any job. The future lies in the man who holds the job.

Liabilities should not affect our assets.

Do more than dream for victory—work for it.

You can't be a winner and be afraid to lose.

Belief is the inner feeling that what we undertake; we can accomplish.

Whether you think you can or think you can't—you're right.

Your chances of success in any undertaking can always be measured by your belief in yourself.

Do the DEED Each Game

Determination: The toughness to do what has to be done.
Effort: Every second will be met with your maximum effort.
Enthusiasm: Play with unbridled joy.
Discipline: The ability to do things the right way.

If you can't win, make the fellow ahead of you break the record

Doubt who you will, but never yourself.

It took us only a few hours to play each game. It will take them a lifetime to forget.

Take time to deliberate, but when the time for action has arrived, stop thinking and go in.

The taboo word is fear. We all deal with it. The difficult part of a game is very short. The amount of time you live with the regret is long.

For God did not give us a spirit of timidity, but a spirit of power, of love and of self-discipline.
                                   2 Timothy 1:7

It is not the critic who counts; not the man who points out how the strong man stumbles, or where the doer of deeds could have done better. The credit belongs to the man who is actually in the arena, whose face is marred by dust and sweat and blood; who strives valiantly, who errs, who comes up short again and again, because there is no effort without error and shortcoming; but who does actually strive to do the deeds; who knows great enthusiasms, the great devotions; who spends himself in a worthy cause; who at the best knows in the end triumph of high achievement and who at the worst, if he fails, at least fails while daring greatly, so that his place shall never be with those cold and timid souls who neither know victory nor defeat.

Theodore Roosevelt

Worry is the misuse of imagination.

The only limit to our realization of tomorrow will be our doubts of today.

Franklin Roosevelt

Courage is the resistance to fear, mastery of fear—not the absence of fear.

Mark Twain

Courage is the capacity to confront what can be imagined.

It is better to have little talent and much purpose than much talent and little purpose.

I never want to leave the court wondering if I did my best. I want to know I did.

Magic Johnson

Obstacles will look large or small to you according to whether you are large or small.

We act or fail to act not because of will but because of imagination.

The people who get on in this world are the people who get up and look for the circumstances they want and if they can't find them, make them.

George Bernard Shaw

If we do what is necessary, all the odds are in our favor.

Let our advance worrying become advance thinking and planning.

Winston Churchill

You don't get what you want, you get what you expect.

I'm always reminding my players to come to every game focused. If you guys can get yourselves to a high level as individuals, I tell them, then I can take you to a higher level as a team. But if you show up a lower lever, I'll have to spend most of my time getting you up to a level you should already have been at.

Mike Krzyzewski

Play like a champion today.

Great minds have purpose—others have wishes.

Take care of the minutes and the hours will take care of themselves.

When I look back on all these worries I remember the story of the old man who said on his deathbed that he had a lot of trouble in his life, most of which never occurred.

Winston Churchill

You cannot discover new oceans unless you have the courage to lose sight of the shore.

Do not allow weaknesses to affect strengths.

I feel sorry for the person who can't get genuinely excited about his work. Not only will he never be satisfied, but he will never achieve anything worthwhile.

Walter Chrysler

Money was never a big motivation for me, except as a way to keep score. The real excitement is playing the game.

Donald Trump

Acting "As If" Boosts Confidence

When you're feeling down—act "as if" you feel confident and in control. By acting it you become it. Athletes can apply the same "as if" principle, especially before the start of competition. Act "as if" you've been there before. For example, if a college freshman is nervous before the start of an important game, tell that athlete to act as if they were still in high school. Remind them that they have to do the same things well to succeed, regardless of the level of competition. Even pretending to act confident can translate into on the field success.

Man is so made that when anything fires his soul, impossibilities vanish. Act enthusiastic and you become enthusiastic.

Dale Carnegie

Make game day your best day.

Make sure you have a clear head when you go into a game. That way, you'll be more likely to react well to whatever unpredictable situation that might occur.

Mike Krzyzewski

Game day is not a day for long, drawn-out speeches. It is a time for interaction.

Mike Krzyzewski

You beat people through execution, you don't beat them because you out jump them, out run them, or outshoot them. You out think them and you out execute them.

Bob Knight

Don't ever allow the pressure of the competition to be greater than the pleasure of the competition.

Here's what I say to myself when I start to feel tense, "Okay, what are you frightened of?"

Jack Nicklaus

Characteristics of being game ready:

- **Relaxed**: The days of getting psyched up are over. Research has shown over and over that the best performances occur when you are just slightly above your normal state of arousal, not the extreme.

- **Confident**: There is no fear. You should expect to be successful, not hope or wish to be successful.

- **Completely focused**: You are oblivious to everything else going on around you—consumed by the moment. Like a child playing with his toys, you are so absorbed in the moment that nothing outside can effect you.

- **Effortless**: Things just sort of happen with little or no effort.

- **Automatic**: There is no interference from your thoughts or emotions. Things are just happening.

- **Fun**: When you having fun its easy

In order to succeed you must know what you're doing, like what you're doing and believe in what you're doing.

Pressure creates tension, and when you're tense you want to get your task over and done with as fast as possible. Never a good thing!

Jack Nicklaus

Risks

To laugh is to risk appearing the fool,
To weep is to risk appearing sentimental,
To reach out for another is to risk involvement,
To expose your feelings is to risk exposing your true self,
To place your ideas and dreams before a crowd is to risk loss,
To love is to risk not being loved in return,
To live is to risk dying,
To hope is to risk despair,
To try is to risk failure.

But risks must be taken, because the greatest risk is to risk nothing.
The person who risks nothing, does nothing, has nothing and is nothing.
Chained by their attitudes, they are a slave, they have forfeited their freedom. Only a person who risks is free.

Action may not always bring happiness, but there is no happiness without action.

Pressure is something you put on yourself and it is a sign of incompetence. If you don't have faith in what you're doing, it's probably because you're not prepared.

Al McGuire

There is no substitute for effort. If someone with superior ability permits you to outwork him you can defeat him. If you permit someone of lesser skill to excel you in effort, he will likely beat you. Always play up to your full potential in every game. The greatest extravagance of all is to waste human potential.

Joe Robbie

Hard work does not always guarantee success, but one thing for sure, you won't succeed without hard work.

If I make a mistake, I'm going to make it aggressively and I'm going to do it quickly.

Bo Schembechler

We play with enthusiasm and recklessness. We aren't afraid to lose. If we win, great. But win or lose, it is the competition that gives us pleasure.

Joe Paterno

Fear is the wicked wand that transforms human beings into vegetables.

Too many people are thinking of security instead of opportunity. They seem more afraid of life than death.

Indecision is fatal. It is better to make a wrong decision than to build up a habit of indecision. If you're wallowing in indecision, you certainly can't act—and action is the basis of success.

Real difficulties can be overcome; it is only the imaginable ones that are unconquerable.

A team wins with the elimination of mistakes and with people who want to win and can't stand losing.
                                    Lou Holtz

You can't afford to be too timid. You have to let yourself go and enjoy the game—not get caught up in the heat of the battle.
                                    Sean Elliot

Worry is evidence of an ill-controlled brain; it is merely a stupid waste of time.

Confidence is courage at ease.

The key is not to tie fun with winning and losing—we already know which is more enjoyable. The true fun comes from competitive pursuit of victory through practice and game. It is that time in any contest when decisions and actions flow unencumbered by mechanics or deep thoughts. The work we put in at practice allows that to happen. But only when we're having fun.
                                    Larry Brown

People who enjoy what they're doing invariable do it well.
                                    Joe Gibbs

Have an impact on every play.

Confidence is the first requisite to great undertakings.

Confidence is that feeling by which the mind embarks on great and honorable courses with a sure hope and trust in itself.

You've got to take the initiative and play your game. In a decisive set, confidence is the difference.
                                    Chris Evert

To succeed in life, you need two things: ignorance and confidence.
                                    Mark Twain

If you have no confidence in yourself, you are twice defeated in the race of life. With confidence, you have won even before you have started.

One who has lost confidence can lose nothing more.

Confidence is contagious. So is lack of confidence. Experience tells you what to do; confidence allows you to do it.

You have to have confidence in your ability, and then be tough enough to follow through. That is why some people with mediocre talent, but with great inner drive, go much further than people with vastly superior talent.

When you have confidence, you can have a lot of fun and when you have fun you can do amazing things.
Joe Namath

If you make every game a life-and-death thing, you're going to have problems. You'll be dead a lot.
Dean Smith

Winning is overrated. The only time it is really important is in surgery and war.
Al McGuire

The essence of sports is that while you're doing it, nothing else matters, but after you stop, there is a place, generally not very important, where you would put it.

There's only one superstition—that it's unlucky to be behind at the end of the game.

To think too long about doing a thing often becomes its undoing.

The best angle from which to approach any problem is the try-angle.

The vision must be followed by the venture. It is not enough to stare up the steps—we must step up the stairs.

Don't be too busy mopping the floor to turn off the faucet.

Vision without action is a daydream. Action with without vision is a nightmare.

All the so-called "secrets of success" will not work unless you do.

You cannot plough a field by turning it over in your mind.

God gives every bird its food, but He does not throw it into its nest.

I've got a theory that if you give 100 percent all of the time, somehow things will work out in the end.

Larry Bird

Nobody ever drowned in his own sweat.

Put your heart, mind, intellect and soul even to your smallest acts. This is the secret of success.

Small deeds done are better than great deeds planned.

All know the way; few actually walk it.

Men expect too much, do too little.

He does not believe who does not live according to his belief.

Winning is not a sometime thing; It's an all time thing. You don't win once in a while, You don't do things right once in a while, you do them right all the time. Winning is a habit, unfortunately so is losing.

Vince Lombardi

To be a great champion you must believe you are the best. If you're not, pretend you are.

Muhammad Ali

Never let the fear of striking out get in the way of knocking one out.

Most games are lost, not won.

The man who cannot believe in himself cannot believe in anything else.

Act as though it were impossible to fail.

A boat is safe in the harbor but that's not what boats are for.

If you are going to take it to the bank, then you better cash it in.

You miss 100 percent of the shots that you don't take.

The only important shot you take is the next one.

Approach the game with no preset agendas and you'll probably come away surprised at your overall efforts.

Phil Jackson

Victory or defeat is not determined at the moment of crisis, but rather in the long and unspectacular period of preparation.

You don't play against an opponent, you play against the game.

Bob Knight

If you're not just a little bit nervous before a match, you probably don't have the expectations of yourself that you should have.

Hale Irwin

Peace of mind is experienced when the stormy waves of the mind quell down.

Inner peace creates outer peace.

True peace of mind is not dependent on circumstances. It comes from the inside.

Worries, fears, desires, restlessness, nervousness drive peace of mind away.

The breakfast of champions is not cereal, it's the opposition.

Practice has put your brains in your muscles.

The thing that separates good players from great ones is mental attitude. It might only make a difference of two or three points in an entire match but how you play those points often makes the difference between winning and losing.

Chris Evert

File Five
After a Win

Very few things are more comforting than a win. But coaches have to be careful that their team doesn't become complacent after winning. Sometimes work habits diminish and players start to get a feeling of arriving when there is still much work to be done. As a coach you have to ensure that your players are focused everyday—especially following a win.

One small breeze does not make a wind storm.

Ego is the drug of stupidity.

He who blows his horn is usually in a big fog.

You're not as good as everyone tells you when you win and you're not as bad as they say when you lose.
Lou Holtz

Do not look back unless you plan to go that way.

We judge ourselves by what we feel capable of doing, while others judge us by what we have already done.

Ability will get you to the top, character determines whether you stay there.

A man has the right to be conceited until he has been successful.

Success has ruined many a man.

The moment of victory is much too short to live for that and nothing else.

Player's attention spans get less and less as they progress.
Mike Krzyzewski

Winning is like a deodorant. It covers up a lot that stinks.
Doc Rivers

The more successful you become, the longer the yardstick becomes that people use to measure you by.
Tom Landry

The time to measure success is when all is said and done; not when there is more to be said and more to be done.

If you let your head get too big, it'll break your neck.

You can have a certain arrogance and that's fine. But never lose respect for others.

Becoming number one is easier than remaining number one.

Don't measure yourself by what you accomplished, but by what you should have accomplished with your ability.

Whenever I say something is 'good enough' it usually isn't.

I always hope I have more desire than accomplishments.

Michelangelo

Never set a goal that involves number of wins—never. Set goals that revolve around playing together as a team. Doing so will put you in a position to win every game.

Mike Krzyzewski

When you stop growing—you start to decay.

Neither criticism nor praise should be highly regarded.

It's always the secure who are humble.

You cannot step into the same river twice.

If what you have done yesterday still looks big to you, you haven't done much today.

Mike Krzyzewski

I don't want to look back. I want to look ahead. I'd hate for my defining moment to be in my past.

Scott Hamilton

Great players never look in the mirror and say I'm a great player. They look in the mirror and say am I the best player I can be?

Michael Jordan

The bigger a man's head gets, the easier it is to fill his shoes.

A moment of ecstasy can cause a lifetime of disappointment.

To be pleased with one's limits is a wretched state.

The toughest thing about success is that you've got to keep on being a success. Talent is only a starting point. You've got to keep on working that talent. Someday you'll reach for it and it won't be there.

Success can make you go one of two ways. It can make you a prima donna, or it can smooth the edges, take away the insecurities, let the nice things come out.

The distance from success to failure is invariably made shorter the longer you cling to a sense of satisfaction.

A great secret of success is to go through life as a man who never gets used up.

The best teams try to fix things when they're winning not after they start to lose.

The problems of victory are more agreeable than the problems of defeat, but they are no less difficult.
                                            Winston Churchill

Nothing fails like success.

The important thing to do after winning is get right back to work. Winning can actually have a negative influence if you become satisfied with yourself. Even in victory, be critical and look for mistakes you have made. Never be completely satisfied. Always search for ways to improve.

Success usually comes to those who are too busy to be looking for it.

Each success only buys an admission ticket to a more difficult problem.

A successful individual sets his next goal above his last achievement.

Those who truly have the spirit of champions are never wholly happy with an easy win. Half the satisfaction stems from knowing that it was the time and the effort you invested that led to your high achievement.

Underpromise; overdeliver.

I know of only one bird—the parrot— that talks; and it can't fly very high.

Don't look back. Something might be gaining on you.
                                            Satchel Paige

Sometimes I worry about being a success in a mediocre world.
                                            Lily Tomlin

Nothing recedes like success.

Don't dwell on reality; it will only keep you from greatness.

If you can count your money, you don't have a billion dollars.

What difference does it make how much you have? What you do not have amounts to much more.

One who is contented with what he has done will never become famous for what he will do.

Never set limits or become too satisfied because limits become limitations and satisfaction leads to a loss of hunger. Stay hungry and keep pushing forward.

He who is contented has lain down to die, and the grass is already over him.

It is right to be contented with what we have, never with what we are.

Fame is proof that people are gullible.

There's a lot to be said for the fellow who doesn't say it himself.

It is easy for a somebody to be modest, but it is difficult to be modest when one is a nobody.

Avoid popularity; it has many snares and no real benefit.

Popular opinion is the greatest lie in the world.

Applause waits on success.
Benjamin Franklin

The hardest tumble a man can make is to fall over his own bluff.

Success has always been a great liar.

The highest form of vanity is love of fame.

We are stripped bare by the curse of plenty.
Winston Churchill

Even if you're on the right track you'll get run over if you just sit there.
Will Rogers

A man wrapped up in himself makes a very small bundle.
Benjamin Franklin

There is always something about your success that displeases even your best friends.
Oscar Wilde

Holding the mile record doesn't make it any easier to run a mile in the future.

You are never better than anyone else until you do something to prove it, and when you are really good you never need to tell anyone. They will tell you.

Success breeds success, but only if you continue to do the things that caused the success in the first place.

You can stand tall without standing on someone. You can be a victor without having victims.

Every morning in Africa, a gazelle wakes up. It knows it must run faster than the fastest lion or it will be killed. Every morning a lion wakes up. It knows it must outrun the slowest gazelle or it will starve to death. It doesn't matter whether you are a lion or a gazelle—when the sun comes up, you'd better be running!

A man's worth should be judged not for getting ahead of others, but by surpassing himself.

You can't get anywhere today if you're bogged down in yesterday.

Cherish yesterday—Dream tomorrow—Live today.

Never measure the height of a mountain until you have reached the top. Then you will see how low it was.

You have thousands of opportunities to keep quiet, use every one of them.

The missing ingredient in most of our talking is a little shortening.

Progress stops upon satisfaction.

Don't bother just to be better than your contemporaries or predecessors. Try to be better than yourself.

Never a horse that couldn't be rode. Never a rider that couldn't be throwed.

Success is reaching your goals, and all else is commentary.

The ability to discipline yourself to delay gratification in the short term in order to enjoy greater rewards in the long term is the indispensable prerequisite for success.

Show me a satisfied man and I'll show you a failure.

The only game to win is the next one.

The two hardest things to handle in life are failures and successes.

There are no speed limits on the road to success.

Persistence is the twin sister of excellence. One is a matter of quality, the other a matter of time.

Mental toughness is the ability to never set limits upon yourself because limits become limitations.

Success has made failures of many men.

File Six

After a Loss

Losing can be trying for the coach as well as the players. However, the coach must maintain his motivation and relay to the team that hope is not lost and there are bigger goals that must be met. The important thing is for one setback not to turn into several losses because of frustration, excuse making, lack of responsibilities or poor individual habits that may creep in. Here are some thoughts to help prevent that from happening.

Never go to bed a loser.

You must have long term goals to keep you from being frustrated by short range failure.

A man is not hurt so much by what happens as by his opinion of what happens.

What happens to a man is less significant than what happens within him.

Experience is not what happens to a man; it is what a man does with what happens to him.

Winning doesn't always mean being first. Winning means you're always doing better than you've ever done before.

There is nothing either good or bad but thinking makes it so.

It's the way we react to circumstances that determines our feelings.

I missed more than 9000 shots in my career. I lost over 300 games. There's been six times I've been trusted to take the game winning shot and missed. I've failed over and over again and that's why I succeed.
Michael Jordan

You take a setback and turn it into a comeback.

Lose faith in yourself and you'll fulfill your worst prophecy.

Victory has a hundred fathers but defeat is an orphan.

Don't brood on what's past but don't forget it either.

Always look at what you have left. Never look at what you have lost.

Nothing is as simple as we hope it will be.

The things which hurt instruct.

A losing team looks for excuses. A championship team looks for solutions.

Jimmy Johnson

Being a sore loser prevents you from getting anything out of a defeat.

You've got to always be aware of why you don't win, otherwise you'll keep losing. Every mistake is a learning experience and the idea is not to make the same mistake again.

It is not the position but the disposition.

It's losing that prepares you to win. Losing helps as long as you don't lose too much.

Mike Krzyzewski

Good judgment comes from experience. Experience comes from bad judgment.

Some defeats are only installments for a later victory.

If at first you don't succeed, you are like most people.

The person who complains about the way the ball bounces is likely the one who dropped it.

You are not judged by the number of times you fail, but by the number of times you succeed; and the number of times you succeed is in direct proportion to the number of times you can fail and keep on trying.

Things turn out best for those who make the best of the way things turned out.

Excuses are the lack of faith in your own power.

Success is never final and failure is never fatal. It is courage that counts.

Winston Churchill

How a man plays a game shows something of his character. How he loses shows all of it.

Do not use a knife to kill a fly on your team's back.

He who wastes today worrying about yesterday will waste tomorrow worrying about today.

The greatest test of courage on the earth is to bear defeat without losing heart.

Even after a bad harvest there must be sowing.

Defeat isn't bitter if you don't swallow it.

You will face many defeats in your life, but never let yourself be defeated.

I am not discouraged because every working attempt discarded is another step forward.

Thomas Edison

We learn wisdom from failure much more than from success. We often discover what we will do by finding out what will not do and probably he who never made a mistake never made a discovery.

What is defeat? Nothing but an education, nothing but the first step to something better.

The boy who is going to make a great man must not make up his mind to overcome a thousand obstacles, but to win in spite of a thousand defeats.

Theodore Roosevelt

Our greatest glory is not in never falling, but in rising every time we fall.

You don't drown by falling in the water; you drown by staying there.

If you can't make a mistake, you can't make anything.

Failure should be our teacher, not our undertaker.

Failure is something we can avoid only by saying nothing, doing nothing, and being nothing.

Failure is only a temporary change in direction to set you straight for your next success.

When defeat comes, accept it as a signal that your plans are not sound, rebuild those plans, and set sail once more toward your coveted goal.

Being defeated is often a temporary condition. Giving up is what makes it permanent.

Men succeed when they realize that their failures are the preparation for their victories.

If you are not big enough to lose, you are not big enough to win.

Failure is an event, never a person.

There is no failure except in no longer trying.

One fails forward toward success.

You should not suffer the past. You should be able to wear it like a loose garment, take it off and let it drop.

Never let yesterday take up too much of today.

When you're a winner you come back no matter what happened the day before.

Never confuse a single defeat with a final defeat.

A failure is a man who has blundered, but is not able to cash in the experience.

There is no failure. Only feedback.

I have always felt that although someone may defeat me, and I strike out in a ball game, the pitcher on the particular day was the best player. But I know when I see him again, I'm going to be ready for his curve ball. Failure is a part of success. There is no such thing as a bed of roses all your life. But failure will never stand in the way of success if you learn from it.

Hank Aaron

You always pass failure on your way to success.

In great attempts, it is glorious even to fail.

Remember your past mistakes just long enough to profit by them.

Failure is success if we learn from it.

Failure will never overtake me if my determination to succeed is strong enough.

Failure is nature's plan to prepare you for great responsibilities.

Failures are like skinned knees, painful but superficial.

I do not fear failure. I only fear the slowing up of the engine inside of me which is pounding, saying, "Keep going, someone must be on top, why not you?

General Patton

Fear of failure must never be a reason not to try something.

Fall seven times, stand up eight.

A stumble may prevent a fall.

Recovering from failure is often easier than building from success.

Failure is the condiment that gives success its flavor.

You're never beaten until you admit it.

Better lose the anchor than the whole ship.

We didn't lose the game; we just ran out of time.
                              Vince Lombardi

If you can't accept losing, you can't win.

Winning is a habit. Unfortunately, so is losing.

Don't give up, don't ever give up.
                              Jim Valvano

Do not be afraid of defeat. You are never so near to victory as when defeated in a good cause.
                              Henry Ward Beecher

Desire and determination must overcome disappointment.
                              Walter Alston

You have class when you can meet triumph and disaster and treat them the same.

You may have to fight a battle more than once to win it.

The true test of individual success is the mirror test. All that matters is if you can look in the mirror and honestly tell the person you see there that you've done your best.

One man practicing sportsmanship is far better than fifty preaching it.

The rewards for perseverance far exceed the pain that goes into persevering.

Great works are performed not by strength but perseverance.

Prefer a loss over a dishonest gain. One brings pain at the moment; the other for all time.

The difference between greatness and mediocrity is often how an individual views a mistake.

If a man has done his best, what else is there?
                              General Patton

Winner vs. Loser

The Winner—is always a part of the answer.

The Loser—is always a part of the problem.

The Winner—always has a purpose.

The Loser—always has an excuse.

The Winner—says "Let me do it for you."

The Loser—says "That's not my job."

The Winner—sees an answer for every problem.

The Loser—sees a problem for every answer.

The Winner—sees a green near every sand trap.

The Loser—sees two or three traps near every green.

The Winner—says, "It may be difficult but it's possible."

The Loser—says, "It may be possible but it's too difficult."

Be a Winner

How much is left in you after you have lost everything outside of you is the true test of your manhood.

Players do their best listening after a loss.

Just because you can do better, it doesn't mean you've done badly.

If you don't fail now and again, it's a sign you're playing it safe.

Believing in yourself is an endless destination, believing you have failed is the end of the journey.

Success is going from failure to failure without a loss of enthusiasm.

You're on the road to success when you realize that failure is only a detour.

Nothing is as good as it seems and nothing is as bad as it seems, but somewhere between is where reality falls.

The harder you fall down, the higher you will bounce up.

A man can make mistakes, but he isn't a failure until he starts blaming someone else.

A man who has committed a mistake and doesn't correct it is committing another mistake.

Ninety-nine percent of the failures come from people who practice the habit of making excuses.

We don't go for the injury bit, the excuse bit. We win or we lose, that's all.

Al McGuire

Falling into the deepest valley is nothing to fear. It just means that you are in the perfect position to climb the world's highest mountain.

Mistakes are a fact of life. It is the response to the error that counts.

Never start talking about if or but or the past because 90 percent of what follows will be negative.

It's never as bad as you think or as good as you think.

Bob Knight

How we play after a loss will determine how good we're going to be.

Others may stop you temporarily but only you can do it permanently.

The easiest thing in sports is to win when you're good. The next easiest thing is to lose when you're not good. The hardest thing, by far, is to lose when you're good. That's the test of character.

File Seven

Before a Big Game—The Rivalry Game

All games are big games, but let's face it, some are bigger than others. Whether it's your cross-town rival or a game for the conference championship, there are some games on the schedule that carry more significance than others. These games can also add a little more weight onto shoulders of the players and coaches. The quotes found here are to help keep the game in perspective and to properly prepare your team for the "big" game.

Some people think they are concentrating when they're merely worrying.

Nothing gives one person so much advantage over another as to remain always cool and unruffled under all circumstances.
                                    Thomas Jefferson

The coolest heads win the hottest games.

The men who try to do something and fail are infinitely better than those who try to do nothing and succeed.

Lack of confidence is born from a lack of preparation.

There is no greater tragedy than doing nothing for fear of doing too little.

There was a lot of emotion at the Alamo and nobody survived.

It's okay to be scared but don't let it dictate your actions.

A good mind has never handicapped a player.

Obstacles are those frightful things you see when you take your eyes off the goal.

Your life is in the hands of any fool who makes you lose your temper.

When I was feeling pressure, I would tell myself that as long as I was a good sport my mom would still love me.
                                    Matt Biondi

Keep your eye on the prize.

When you lose control of your emotions, when your self-discipline breaks down, your judgment and common sense suffer. How can you perform at your best when you are using poor judgment?

Mentally tough athletes respond to emotion with technique—not emotion.

Courage is doing what you're afraid to do. There can be no courage unless you're scared.

I never prepared my teams to play a certain team each week. I prepared them to play anybody. I didn't want my players worrying about the other fellas. I wanted them executing the sound offensive and defensive principles we taught in practice.
John Wooden

Only those who dare to fail greatly can ever achieve greatly.

You can't change because circumstances around you change.

Concentration is the ability to think about absolutely nothing when it is absolutely necessary.

Pray for a good harvest, but keep on plowing.

There is a time to let things happen and a time to make things happen.

You cannot depend on your eyes when your imagination is out of focus.
Mark Twain

A mind troubled by doubt cannot focus on the course to victory.

The ability to focus attention on important things is a defining characteristic of intelligence.

Energy is the essence of life. Every day you decide how you're going to use it by knowing what you want and what it takes to reach that goal, and by maintaining focus.

Focus 90 percent of your time on solutions and only 10 percent of your time on problems.

Concentration comes out of a combination of confidence and hunger.

As in love, too much concentration on technique can often lead to impotence.

One of the symptoms of an approaching nervous breakdown is the belief that one's work is terribly important.

Learn the fundamentals of the game and stick to them. Band-Aid remedies never last.

Great deeds are usually wrought at great risks.

The eye of a human being is a microscope, which makes the world seem bigger than it really is.

To the man who only has a hammer in the toolkit, every problem looks like a nail.

You can discover what your enemy fears most by observing the means he uses to frighten you.

Fear is that little darkroom where negatives are developed.

Focus on the journey, not the destination. Joy is found not in finishing an activity but in doing it.

As long as you keep your focus, your destination is obtainable.

Success is focusing the full power of all you are on what you have a burning desire to achieve.

Courage means to keep working, to continue seeking solutions to difficult problems, and to stay focused during stressful periods.

No life ever grows until it is focused, dedicated, disciplined.

Only when your consciousness is totally focused on the moment you are in can you receive whatever gift, lesson, or delight that moment has to offer.

What do I mean by concentration? I mean focusing totally on the business at hand and commanding your body to do exactly what you want it to do.

Arnold Palmer

Concentration, confidence, competitive urge, capacity for enjoyment. My concentration level blocks out everything. Concentration is why some athletes are better than others. You develop that concentration in training.

Edwin Moses

The ability to concentrate and to use time well is everything.

Concentrate on your job and you will forget your other troubles.

It is those who can concentrate on but one thing at a time who advance in this world.

The great man or woman is the one who never steps outside his or her specialty or foolishly dissipates his or her individuality.

My ability to concentrate and work toward that goal has been my greatest asset.

Jack Nicklaus

Concentrate on concentrating.

Success in life is a matter not so much of talent as of concentration and perseverance.

Do not dwell in the past, do not dream of the future, concentrate the mind on the present moment.

The winners in life think constantly in terms of I can, I will, and I am. Losers, on the other hand, concentrate their waking thoughts on what they should have or would have done, or what they can't do.

You can do only one thing at a time. Simply tackle one problem and concentrate all efforts on what you are doing at the moment.

Enter every activity without giving mental recognition to the possibility of defeat.

Concentrate on your strengths, instead of your weaknesses—on your powers, instead of your problems.

Every great player has learned the two C's—how to concentrate and how to maintain composure.

The best way of forgetting how you think you feel is to concentrate on what you know you know.

Four things that help maintain composure when dealing with a tough situation:

1. Stick to the fundamentals—It's the basics that will get you through—not the spectacular.
2. Stay in the moment—Don't let emotions from similar situations or experiences transfer to the current situation.
3. Accept what you cannot change; change what you can.
4. Keep it real—don't try to fake out your feelings. Accept them and enjoy them.

Many people lose their tempers merely from seeing you keep yours.

Nothing baffles the schemes of evil people so much as the calm composure of great souls.

Believe in miracles but don't depend on them.

Trust yourself. You know more than you think you do.

Don't think, just do.

Start by doing what's necessary, then do what's possible, and suddenly you are doing the impossible.

When things are steep, remember to stay level-headed.

If you're going to look back on something and enjoy it, you might as well enjoy it now.

In calmness there should be activity; in activity there should be calmness.

Calmness of mind is one of the beautiful jewels of wisdom.

Nothing is so aggravating than calmness.

The pursuit, even of the best things, ought to be calm and tranquil.

Calmness is the cradle of power.

One cool judgment is worth a thousand hasty counsels.

Supply light and not heat.

The world belongs to the enthusiast who keeps cool.

Doomed are the hotheads! Unhappy are they who lose their cool and are too proud to say, "I'm sorry."

Keep cool; anger is not an argument.

Keep cool and you will command everyone.

Calmness is the ideal state in which we should receive all life's experiences. Nervousness is the opposite of calmness, and its prevalence today makes it very nearly a world disease.

Concentration is having a one pointed mind.

Always behave like a duck—keep calm and unruffled on the surface but paddle like the devil underneath.

This should be a man's attitude— Few things will disturb him at all; nothing will disturb him much.

Maintain your composure—the worst thing you can do to an opponent is to beat him.

Don't lose your head. It's the best part of your body.

Anger is never without reason—but seldom a good one.

Play the golf course—not the opponent.

                    Dean Smith

If you chase two rabbits, both will escape.

Focus: The sharper it is, the sharper you are.

File Eight

When You're the Favorite

One of the toughest tasks for any coach is to get his players ready for a game in which they are the favorite. Whether it against a team you have already beaten or a team in the bottom portion of the standings, getting players ready for these games is much harder than the big games. Here are some thoughts to help get your team ready for games they think they're supposed to win.

Mental toughness is the ability to push yourself to a point and once you reach it still want to go on.

Believe you can win but have respect for the fact that you can always lose.

Focus on competition has always been a formula for mediocrity.

Here's a good rule of thumb; too clever is dumb.

The man of genius is he and he alone who finds such joy in his art that he will work at it come hell or high water.

Only the race in which you're in is important.

Play every game like you just lost your last game.

Self-conceit may lead to self-destruction.

It is a very bad thing to become accustomed to good luck.

Talent is God-given—be humble. Faith is man-given—be grateful. Conceit is self-given—be careful.
John Wooden

In order to hit a good golf shot at the moment in time you're standing over the ball, you have to believe that golf shot is the most important thing in the world.
Tiger Woods

The only thing that comes without effort is old age.

Shooting below par today doesn't guarantee below par tomorrow.

Never trust the umpire when you have two strikes.

When they discover the center of the universe, a lot of people will be disappointed to discover they are not it.

A lot of people level off and let their own performance standards dominate them instead of seeking higher levels of competition. They never really find out how good they can be.
John Wooden

The smaller the mind, the greater the conceit.

Conceit is God's gift to little men.

It is impossible for anyone to begin to learn that which he thinks he already knows.

The greatest of faults is to be conscious of none.

I want our team to constantly play as if they have got something to prove to people.
John Thompson

The secret to success is to keep a firm grip on the situation and treat each match the same.
Ivan Lendel

Life is a long lesson in humility.

You can't build a reputation on what you are going to do.

A good name, like good will, is got by many actions and lost by one.

We can draw lessons from the past, but we cannot live in it.

Live neither in the past nor in the future, but let each day's work absorb your entire energies, and satisfy your wildest ambition.

Events in the past may be roughly divided into those which probably never happened and those which do not matter.

Conceit is an insuperable obstacle to all progress.

Conceit spoils the finest genius.

To be scared is sensible, to be comfortable is suicidal.

See the man wise in his own conceit? There is more hope for a fool than for him.
Proverbs 26:7

Always hold your head up but be careful to keep your nose at a friendly level.

He who is enamored of himself will at least have the advantage of being inconvenienced by few rivals.

Whatever accomplishment you boast of in the world, there is someone better than you.

Conceit in weakest bodies works the strongest.

Conceit is bragging about yourself. Confidence means you believe you can get the job done.

Conceit is a strange disease—it makes everyone sick except the person who has it.

As long as I have a want, I have a reason for living. Satisfaction is death.

Whether you find satisfaction in life depends not on your tale of years, but on your will.

Lots of people know how to be successful, but very few people know how to handle success.

Chance favors the prepared team—not the team that's favored.

Consistency requires you to be as ignorant today as you were a year ago.

The secret of success is consistency of purpose.

Winning is not a sometime thing—you don't win once in a while. You win all the time.
                                    Vince Lombardi

It is what the race means to you that determines how hard you run it.

Greatness is not attained by accumulating victories—it is attained by chasing the next one.

Pride never allows you to take a day off when there is work to be done.

A champion's thirst is never quenched.

File Nine

When You're the Underdog

It's challenging to prepare for a game in which you are not the favorite. On one hand it can provide a huge motivational boost for your team, while on the other hand it can lead to a feeling of insecurity and a lack of confidence. Many teams are beaten before they step on the playing field because of preconceived notions or because of what happened in a previous game. Here are some words of advice to help prepare your team when they are the underdog.

The harder the conflict, the more glorious the triumph.

Skating on thin ice is better than skating on no ice at all.

A small man can be just as exhausted as a great man.

Doubt whom you will but never yourself.

Success is doing what it takes in spite of one's fears.

Of positive and negative thoughts— it doesn't cost one cent more to think positively.

Overcome resistance with persistence.

If you find a path with no obstacles, it probably doesn't lead anywhere.

Champions know it's not having the talent to win that makes a champion; it's having too much pride to lose.

Our greatest weakness lies in giving up. The most certain way to succeed is to always try just one more time.

I'd rather attempt to do something great and fail, than attempt to do nothing and succeed.

Mental toughness is the ability to avoid all negative foresight because foresight be it winning or losing too often becomes a reality.

Impossible is a word to be found only in the dictionary of fools.

Free your mind of can't.

We often give the enemy the means for our own destruction.

You can never succeed until you believe you will succeed.

The strongest factor in prosperity is self-esteem; believing you can do it, believing you deserve it, believing you will get it.

What the mind can achieve and believe, the body can achieve.

Sometimes we are so afraid of hitting bad shots we don't let ourselves hit good ones.
                                    Butch Harmon

It's okay to be a pessimist because of your intelligence but also be an optimist because of your will.

Having fun is doing hard things well.

The impossible is what nobody can do until someone does it.

Remember you meet your opponents and not their reputations.

Thinking about the devil is worst than seeing the devil.
                                    Branch Rickey

It is a funny thing about life, if you refuse to accept anything but the best, you very often will get it.

Our life is what our thoughts make it.

Failures are divided into two classes—those who thought and never did, and those who did and never thought.

A normal reaction to an idea is to think of reasons why it cannot be done.

Concentrate on where you want to go, not on what you fear.

No one can make you feel inferior without your consent.

All goals set with a firm belief and commitment are attainable.

The more we fail, the greater our chance of succeeding.

Every great achievement was once considered impossible.

If you want success, start thinking of yourself as a success.

Never give up on what you really want to do.

The person with big dreams is more powerful than one with all the facts.

Courage does not always roar. Sometimes courage is the small quiet voice at the end of the day saying, "I will try again tomorrow."

Keep away from people who try to belittle your ambitions. Small people always do that, but the really great make you feel that you too can become great.

> Nothing in the world can take the place of persistence. Talent will not; nothing is more common than unsuccessful men with talent. Genius will not; unrewarded genius is almost a proverb. Education will not; the world is full of educated derelicts. Persistence and determination alone are omnipotent. The slogan press on has solved and always will solve the problems of the human race.
>
> Calvin Coolidge

As long as you're going to think anyway—you might as well think BIG.

Nothing big ever came from being small.

Success in life comes not from holding a good hand, but in playing a poor hand well.

All of us have at least one great voice deep inside. People are products of their environments. A lucky few are born into situations in which positive message abound. Others grow up hearing too many messages of fear and failure, which they must block out, so the positive can be heard. But the positive and courageous voice will always emerge, somewhere, sometime, for all of us. Listen for it and your breakthrough will come.

Pat Riley

One man with courage is a majority.

He who loses wealth loses much; he who loses a friend loses more; but he that loses courage loses all.

A great pleasure in life is doing what people say you cannot do.

We are continually faced by great opportunities brilliantly described as unsolvable problems.

There's no thrill in easy sailing when the skies are clear and blue

There's no joy in merely doing the things which any one can do

But there is much satisfaction that is mighty sweet to take when you reach a destination that you thought you'd never make.

Use the past as a springboard, not a sofa.

Have the courage to face a difficulty lest it kick you harder than you bargained for.

Only those who will risk going too far can possibly find out how far one can go.

Everyone has a talent. What is rare is the courage to follow the talent to the dark place where it leads.

You have to accept whatever comes and the only important thing is that you meet it with courage and the best you have to give.

Mental toughness is what separates players. Some players are so weak mentally that even the slightest bit of discomfort will distract them from their goal. And some are so strong that nothing that happens to them will distract them.

To play well, you must be mentally aggressive. Instead of worrying about failing—about stopping the shooter and what he might do—my attitude is that he has to beat me.
Kevin Johnson

Talent does not win games; desire wins games.

There comes a time when a man must stop backing down and step forward and meet a challenge; otherwise he's not much of a man.

Learn to look back to learn from your mistakes and learn to look forward with confidence.

There's a difference between becoming frustrated and playing frustrated.

Any goal lightly set is easily abandoned at the first sign of difficulty.

Winners expect to win in advance.

It's not what you think you are that holds you back. It's what you think you are not.

Courage is fear that has said its prayers.

Courage is the art of being the only one who knows you're scared to death.

I wanted you to see what real courage is, instead of getting the idea that courage is a man with a gun in his hand. It's when you know you're licked before you begin but you begin anyway and you see it through no matter what.

To Kill a Mockingbird

A timid person is frightened before a danger, a coward during the time, and a courageous person afterward.

Courage is being scared to death— but saddling up anyway.

John Wayne

A hero is no braver than an ordinary man, but he is braver five minutes longer.

Keep your fears to yourself, but share your courage with others.

Come to the edge.
"We can't. We're afraid."
Come to the edge.
"We can't. We will fall!"
Come to the edge.
 And they came.
 And he pushed them.
 And they flew.

It is not because things are difficult that we do not dare, it is because we do not dare that they are difficult.

Take the first step in faith. You don't have to see the whole staircase, just take the first step.

I tell you the truth, if you have faith as small as a mustard seed, you can say to this mountain, move from here to there and it will move.

Matthew 17:20

Courage is not the absence of fear, but rather the judgment that something else is more important than fear.

Most of the important things in the world have been accomplished by people who have kept on trying when there seemed to be no hope at all.

Courage, above all things, is the first quality of a warrior.

Courage is never to let your actions be influenced by your fears.

Only be you strong, and very courageous, then you will make your way prosperous, and then you will have good success.

Joshua 1:7-8

There are no maps to where no one has gone before.

If Columbus had turned back, no one would have blamed him. Of course, no one would have remembered him either.

Anyone can hold the helm when the sea is calm.

Nothing ventured, nothing gained.

The person who removes a mountain begins by carrying away small stones.

A hero is one who knows how to hang on one minute longer.

Reach for the moon, even if you miss you'll be among the stars.

Train your head and hands to do, your head and heart to dare.

Only those who dare to fail greatly can achieve greatly.

Robert F. Kennedy

It is better to live one day as a lion, than a thousand days as a lamb.

Live your own life, for you will die your own death.

All serious daring starts from within.

And the trouble is if you don't risk anything, you risk even more.

Some succeed because they are destined to, but most succeed because they are determined to.

The ultimate measure of a man is not where he stands in moments of comfort and convenience, but where he stands at times of challenge and controversy.

It is not the size of the dog in the fight but the size of the fight in the dog.

Every time you meet a situation, though you think at the time it is an impossibility and you go through the tortures of the damned, once you have met it and lived through it, you find that forever after you are freer than you were before.

Eleanor Roosevelt

Take a chance! All life is a chance. The man who goes the furthest is generally the one who is willing to do and dare. The sure thing boat never gets far from shore.

Challenges are what make life interesting; overcoming them is what makes life meaningful.

Don't be afraid your life will end; be afraid that it will never begin.

Most of the important things in the world have been accomplished by people who have kept on trying when there seemed to be no hope at all.

It takes a lot of courage to release the familiar and seemingly secure, to embrace the new. But there is no real security in what is no longer meaningful. There is more security in the adventurous and exciting, for in movement there is life, and in change there is power.

Yesterday I dared to struggle—today I dare to win.

I would rather fail in a cause that will ultimately triumph than to triumph in a cause that will ultimately fail

Dare to be naive.

Only when we are no longer afraid do we begin to live.

Worry never robs tomorrow of its sorrow, it only saps today of its joy.

You can measure a man by the opposition it takes to discourage him.

Fear is only as deep as the mind allows.

Feed your faith and your fears will starve to death.

Forget past mistakes. Forget failures. Forget about everything except what you're going to do now—and do it.

The mighty oak was once a little nut that stood its ground.

Worrying is like a rocking chair: it gives you something to do, but it doesn't get you anywhere.

Nurture your mind with great thoughts, for you will never go any higher than you think.

Courage is like a muscle; it is strengthened by use.

No one reaches a high position without daring.

The one permanent emotion of the inferior man is fear—fear of the unknown, the complex, the inexplicable. What he wants beyond everything else is safety.

Life is a compromise of what your ego wants to do, what experience tells you to do, and what nerves let you do.

All problems become smaller if you don't dodge them, but confront them.

Touch a thistle timidly, and it pricks you; grasp it boldly, and its spines crumble.

It is better to die on one's feet than to live on one's knees.

Cowardice is almost always simply a lack of ability to suspend the functioning of the imagination.

There comes a time in every man's life when you have to grow up, accept responsibility and kick some ass.

Pat Riley

Beaten paths are for beaten men.

The greater the obstacle, the greater the glory in overcoming it.

You can get disgusted, but you should never get discouraged.

Stand up to your obstacles and do something about them. You will find that they haven't half the strength you think they have.

It's never an upset if the so-called underdog has all along considered itself the better team.

Fear comes from uncertainty. When we are absolutely certain, whether of our worth or worthlessness, we are almost impervious to fear.

In times of stress, be bold and valiant.

What you are afraid to do is a clear indicator of the next thing you need to do.

Those who live in the past are generally afraid to compete in the present.

If we could be heroes, if just for one day.

One must think like a hero merely to behave like a decent human being.

What worries you, masters you.

Doubt breeds doubt.

If you keep on saying things are going to be bad, you have a good chance of becoming a prophet.

It is better to light a candle than to curse the darkness.

We cannot do everything at once, but we can do something at once.

Don't worry about losing—think about winning.

If there exists no possibility of failure, then victory is meaningless.

File Ten

Overcoming Adversity

Within every season there are difficult times that come along. It may be an injury to a key player, sickness or another type of misfortune that occurs. Successful teams handle adversity. As the coach you have to make sure your players don't use adversity as an excuse. Here are some thoughts to help overcome hard times.

Tough times don't last, tough people do.

Never let problems or circumstances get in the way. You decide that there is always a way to succeed if you're really committed.

There is no education like adversity.

Mental toughness is the ability to accept a situation, be it positive or negative while realizing there is a big difference between accepting and being satisfied.

The greater part of our happiness or misery depends on our dispositions and not our circumstances.

When it's dark enough you can see all the stars.

Sometimes you're the pigeon and sometimes you're the statue.

Adversity cause some men to break—others to break records.

The crisis of yesterday is the joke of tomorrow.

About the time we think we can make ends meet, somebody moves the ends.

You may not be able to control the winds, but you can adjust the sails.

Mental toughness is the ability to avoid excuses.

Character is not built in an emergency—merely exhibited.

It's how we react to events, not the events themselves, that determine our attitudes.

An alibi is like a crutch. It is only for the lame and weak.

Mental toughness is the ability to never have self-sympathy. Sympathy should always be reserved for those who really need it.

To fly we have to have resistance.

When fate closes a door, go through a window.

The grass is not always greener on the other side of the fence. Fences have nothing to do with it. Grass is greener where it is watered. In other words, water and tend to the grass wherever you are.

To appreciate heaven well, tis good for a man to have some 15 minutes of hell.

The best luck to have been born with is the ability and determination to overcome bad luck.

Don't pray when it rains if you don't pray when the sun shines.

When you have the attitude of a champion, you see adversity as your training partner.

Not being able to govern events, I govern myself, and apply myself to them, if they will not apply themselves to me.

If you want the rainbow, you gotta put up with the rain.

Don't dwell on what went wrong. Instead, focus on what to do next.

In attacking adversity, only a positive attitude, alertness, and regrouping to basics can launch a comeback.

The positive things we do that bring about positive results must be present regardless of the situation.

Anyone can stand tall on the high peaks. It's the people who survive the valleys between the peaks that emerge the strongest.

What separates the winners from the losers is how a person reacts to each new twist of fate.
                                        Donald Trump

Pain is inevitable, suffering is optional.

Mental toughness is the ability to look beyond the present for a more desirable situation while realizing what it takes to get there.

Nothing is good or bad, but thinking makes it so.

Internal feelings and approach should not change just because the circumstances do.

Strong determination to succeed tends to supersede anything that could be a potential obstacle.

Commitment is discovered in the midst of adversity.

Sometimes adversity can work in your favor. Instead of feeling sorry for yourself and using it as an excuse, accept the situation and try to make the most of it. That's how a team develops resilience and character.
Mike Krzyzewki

A certain amount of opposition is of great help to a man. Kites rise against, not with the wind.

A dose of adversity is often as needful as a dose of medicine.

A pessimist sees the difficulty in every opportunity; an optimist sees the opportunity in every difficulty.

Adversity reveals genius, prosperity conceals it.

Adversity has the effect of eliciting talents, which, in prosperous circumstances, would have lain dormant.

It doesn't make any difference whether what you face is something that affects your work, your personal relationships, your sense of security, your appraisal of self-worth, or your appearance—the way you think about your situation largely determines whether you will do anything about it and what you will do.

The gem cannot be polished without friction.

Adversity introduces a man to himself.

There is no greater sorrow than to recall a happy time in the midst of wretchedness.

If you break your neck, if you have nothing to eat, if your house is on fire, then you've got a problem. Everything else is an inconvenience.

If you're going through hell, keep going.
Winston Churchill

We have no right to ask when sorrow comes, "Why did this happen to me?" unless we ask the same question for every moment of happiness that comes our way.

A bend in the road is not the end of the road—unless you fail to make the turn.

I know God will not give me anything I can't handle. I just wish that He didn't trust me so much.
                                    Mother Teresa

The only thing that overcomes hard luck is hard work.

When we acquire the strength we have overcome.

I ask not for a lighter burden, but for broader shoulders.

Birds sing after a storm; why shouldn't people feel as free to delight in whatever happens to them?

Turn your wounds into wisdom.

Sometimes the littlest things in life are the hardest to take. You can sit on a mountain more comfortably than on a tack.

How can something bother you if you won't let it?

It just wouldn't be a picnic without the ants.

If you don't like something change it—if you can't change it, change the way you think about it.

The problem is not that there are problems. The problem is expecting otherwise and thinking that having problems is a problem.

Every path has its puddle.

I believe there are more urgent and honorable occupations than the incomparable waste of time we call suffering.

He who has a why to live can bear almost any how.

We survive every moment, after all, except the last one.

The difficulties of life are intended to make us better, not bitter.

Doing what's right is no guarantee against misfortune.

The turning point in the process of growing up is when you discover the core of strength within you that survives all hurt.

Everybody ought to do at least two things each day that he hates to do, just for practice.

Past and to come, seems best; things present, worse.
                    William Shakespeare

There are times in everyone's life when something constructive is born out of adversity—when things seem so bad that you've got to grab your fate by the shoulders and shake it.

The darkest hour has only sixty minutes.

God gave burdens, also shoulders.

Problems are the price you pay for progress.

When you're feeling your worst, that's when you get to know yourself the best.

If the wind will not serve, take to the oars.

No man is more unhappy than the one who is never in adversity; the greatest affliction of life is never to be afflicted.

That which does not kill us makes us stronger.

No pressure, no diamonds.

When one door closes another opens. But we often look so long and so regretfully upon the closed door that we do not see the one which has opened for us.

The child's philosophy is a true one. He does not despise the bubble because it burst; he immediately sets to work to blow another one.

Only in the winter can you tell which trees are truly green. Only when the winds of adversity blow can you tell whether an individual has courage and steadfastness.
                    John F. Kennedy

A clever man reaps some benefit from the worst catastrophe and a fool can turn even good luck to his disadvantage.

The purest ore is produced in the hottest furnace and the brightest thunderbolt is elicited from the darkest storm.

Let what will come. You can receive
no damage from it unless you think
it a calamity and it is in your power
to think it is none if you so decide.

The successful man lengthens his
stride when he discovers that the
signpost has deceived him; the
failure looks for a place to sit down.

Some people are so fond of bad luck
they run half way to meet it.

File Eleven

Midseason Doldrums & Avoiding Slumps

Midseason doldrums. We hope they never come but there are times when a team faces a slump. Players can lose enthusiasm and unless you have committed people in your program, they begin to tire of the daily routine. One key to success is to keep your team focused through the middle part of the season and avoid any type of slump. It's easier to get your team excited at the beginning of the season and at playoff time. The challenge is to keep them excited during the middle of the season or if they hit a slump. Slumps often cause you to reevaluate and try new things. They can also cause players to lose enthusiasm and go away from the things they need to do to be successful. Here are some thoughts to help prevent that from happening.

It is a case of give and take in this world—with not enough people willing to give what it takes.

Winners forget they're in a race—they just love to run.

Achievers sacrifice, struggle, work on, perhaps alone, weary and discouraged and yet at each step overcome the negative.

You work your whole life to be the best you can be even if it's only for one day or one week.

Don't throw away the old bucket until you know whether the new one holds water.

Teams do not go physically flat—they go mentally stale.
                                        Vince Lombardi

People don't win because they're physically stronger. They win because they're stronger between the ears.

You become a champion step-by-step—not by leaps and bounds.

Half the failures of this world come from pulling in one's horse as he is leaping.

The individual activity of one man with backbone will do more than a thousand men with a mere wishbone.

Winning is great but it's the long road to get there that makes it worthwhile.

He who stops getting better stops being good.

Build momentum by accumulating small successes.

It's worst still to be ignorant of your ignorance.

Never quit. As the Russian proverb states—pray to God but keep rowing to shore.

To change how you feel, you've got to change your physiology—your breathing, your posture, your movements, your facial expressions—everything.

Practice without improvement is meaningless.

Change the intensity of a negative situation by using positive words.

A man does not stay defeated because of something that happens to him, but within him.

Tears will get you sympathy; sweat will get you change.

For all sad words of tongue and pen, the saddest are these—it might have been.

The harder you work, the luckier you get.

A mind free of negatives produces positives.

Our life is what our thoughts make it.

Never rate potential over performance.

The mark of a good team is how it reacts when things aren't going in its favor.

The great thing in this world is not so much where we stand as in what direction we are moving.

It's what you learn after you know it all that counts.
                                John Wooden

It's not enough to be industrious; so are the ants. The question is what are you industrious about?

Not doing more than the average is what keeps you average.

If you're through learning, you're through.

Nothing great was ever achieved without enthusiasm.
                        Ralph Waldo Emerson

Ignorance on fire is better than knowledge on ice.

It is not only what you do, but also what you did not do, for which you are accountable.

When things go bad don't go with them.

When things go bad it is usually mental not physical.

Character, in the long run, is the decisive factor in the life of an individual.

Men can starve from a lack of self-realization as much as they can from a lack of bread.

The worst bankrupt in the world is the person who has lost his enthusiasm.

There's no such thing as coulda, shoulda, woulda. If you should and coulda, you woulda done it.

One man has enthusiasm for 30 minutes, another for 30 days, but it is the man who has it for 30 years who makes a success of his life.

He is great who can do what he wishes; he is wise who wishes to do what he can.

A wise man will make more opportunities than he finds.

When your team is winning, be ready to be tough, because winning can make you soft. On the other hand, when you team is losing, stick by them. Keep believing.
                Bo Schembechler

Losing streaks are funny. If you lose at the beginning, you get off to a bad start. If you lose in the middle of the season, you're in a slump. If you lose at the end, you're choking.
                Gene Mauch

There are only two things I had to do to win the Olympic gold: Train when I wanted to, and train when I didn't.
                Peter Vidmar

If you only work on days you feel good, you won't get much accomplished in life.

Practice as if you were to play forever. Play as if you were to die tomorrow.

Plenty of men can do good work for a spurt and with immediate promotion in mind, but for promotion you want a man in whom good work has become a habit.

Look at the things you do each day and ask yourself why you're doing them. Is it because they're familiar and comfortable and secure? Are you anxious about venturing outside of your cozy comfort zone? Are there things you avoid doing because they might cause you some discomfort? Accomplishment requires that you step outside of your comfort zone. The good news is that when you venture beyond the borders, your comfort zone expands. Success in one area will give you more confidence in everything you do.

Excellence—going far beyond that call of duty, doing more than others expect...this is what excellence is all about. And it comes from striving, maintaining the highest standards, looking after the smallest detail, and going the extra mile. Excellence means doing your very best—in everything; in everyway.

Anyone can start a marathon; the only ones who count are the ones who finish.

What's more important than what you're doing is how you're doing it.

I refuse to accept less than what I'm capable of achieving at any time. My goal for every game is to play better than the one before.
David Robinson

Being successful is a lot like climbing a mountain. The closer you get to the top, the more effort you must exert.

If you know what you want to do—do it now. There are only so many tomorrows.

Any man's life will be filled with constant and unexpected encouragement if he makes up his mind to do his level best each day.

Celebrate what you want to see more of.

Set a man a fire and he'll be warm for a night. Set a man ON fire and he'll be warm for the rest of his life.

You can't light a fire with a wet match.

A man can succeed at almost anything for which he has unlimited enthusiasm.

A mediocre idea that generates enthusiasm will go further than a great idea that inspires no one.

No man is sane who does not know how to be insane on proper occasions.

None are so old as those who have outlived enthusiasm.

I prefer the errors of enthusiasm to the indifference of wisdom.

If you are not getting as much from life as you want to, then examine the state of your enthusiasm.

Enthusiasm is the yeast that raises the dough.

Take pride in how far you have come; have faith in how far you can go.

People may forget how long it took to do the job but they'll never forget how well you did the job.

A champion is one who gets up when he can't.

The future depends on what we do in the present.

Men do less than they ought, unless they do all they can.

Yesterday is a canceled check. Tomorrow is a promissory note. Today is all the cash you have. Spend it wisely.

The value of life lies not in the length of days, but in the use we make of them.

You may delay, but time will not.

Slump? I ain't in no slump. I just ain't hittin.
Yogi Berra

All winning teams are goal-oriented. Teams like these win consistently because everyone connected with them concentrates on specific objectives. They go about their business with blinders on; nothing will distract them from achieving their aims.

Slump, and the world slumps with you. Push, and you push alone.

My motto was always to keep swinging. Whether I was in a slump or feeling badly or having trouble off the field, the only thing to do was keep swinging.
Hank Aaron

It's only a hitch when you're in a slump. When you're hitting the ball, it's called rhythm.
> Eddie Mathews

Enthusiasm—the sustaining power of all great action.

Success generally depends upon knowing how long it will take to succeed.

If you aren't fired with enthusiasm, you will be fired with enthusiasm.
> Vince Lombardi

Great works are performed not by strength but by perseverance.

Fires can't be made with dead embers, nor can enthusiasm be stirred by spiritless men. Enthusiasm in our daily work lightens effort and turns even labor into pleasant tasks.

If everything seems under control, you're just not going fast enough.

Apathy can be overcome by enthusiasm, and enthusiasm can only be aroused by two things: first, an idea, with takes the imagination by storm, and second, a definite intelligible plan for carrying that idea into practice.

There is a real magic in enthusiasm. It spells the difference between mediocrity and accomplishment.

Knowledge is power and enthusiasm pulls the switch.

When an individual fear or apathy passes by the unfortunate, life is of no account.

Nobody who ever gave his best regretted it.

It's a little like wrestling a gorilla. You don't quit when you're tired— you quit when the gorilla is tired.

If you aren't playing well, the game isn't as much fun. When that happens, I tell myself just to go out and play as I did when I was a kid.

Do you know what my favorite part of the game is? The opportunity to play everyday.
> Mike Singletary

Most people never run far enough on their first wind to find out they've got a second.

The successful person makes a habit of doing what the failing person doesn't like to do.

You must get good at one of two things: sowing in the spring or begging in the fall.

To succeed in life in today's world, you must have the will and tenacity to finish the job.

It has been my observation that most people get ahead during the time that others waste time.

If you are bored with life, if you don't get up every morning with a burning desire to do things—you don't have enough goals.

Lou Holtz

A free lunch is only found in mousetraps.

Do a little more each day than you think you possibly can.

Do every act of your life as if it were your last.

You don't get paid for the hour. You get paid for the value you bring to the hour.

The cure for boredom is curiosity.

When people are bored, it is primarily with their own selves that they are bored.

Boredom: the desire for desires.

Boredom flourishes when you feel safe. It's a symptom of security.

Being bored is an insult to oneself.

Boredom is the feeling that everything is a waste of time; serenity, that nothing is.

Boredom is a sickness the cure for which is work.

You must succeed on your own personal motivation, dedication, and commitment—you must have the mindset of: if you're not out there training, someone else is.

Slumps are like a soft bed. They're easy to get into and hard to get out of.

Every day you guys look worse and worse. And today you played like tomorrow.

Nothing is wonderful when you get used to it. That's why you have keep accepting new challenges.

I hated every minute of training but I said don't quit. Suffer now and live the rest of your life as a champion.
                              Muhammad Ali

Pride is not a coat; it's not something that you lay down for two or three days and then decide when you get up some morning that you'll have pride that day and put it on. It must be there every day and it takes constant work to achieve it, to keep it.

People seldom want to walk over you until you lie down.

Success is a matter not so much of talent as of concentration and perseverance.

File Twelve

Dealing With Problems

Problems—we don't want them but we all get them. It could be an upset parent, player or something worse—team dissension. If you coach long enough, you find yourself having to deal with situations that you'd rather not have to deal with. Keep a firm grip on the situation and use the following words of wisdom to help get through the predicament.

The coach is the only person who will tell the players the truth about how they are playing. Friends and family will not.

The hardest thing to learn in life is which bridge to cross and which bridge to burn.

A successful man is one who can lay a firm foundation with the bricks others have thrown at him.

The coach who says he likes criticism should be happy most of the time.

If you are not criticized, you may not be doing much.

Champions never complain, they are too busy getting better.

Sports do not build character—they reveal it.

The man who can't dance thinks the band is no good.

Most people when they think they are thinking are merely rearranging their prejudices.

If a problem has no solution, it may not be a problem, but a fact—not to be solved, but to be coped with over time.

One day a few years ago, a parent accused a coach of having favorites on his team. Several other parents nodded their heads in agreement. The implications were that this was a terrible sin. When he was a younger coach, he probably would have let it get to him and tell them he didn't play favorites. Instead he responded "Yes, I do have favorites. My favorites are those athletes who most passionately did what I asked of them." Those that did, he gave more attention to. Too often coaches spend more time dealing with players that don't do what they're asked and the wrong message is relayed.

If you're busy rowing the boat, you won't have time to rock it.

The more you complain, the more you find things to complain about. The more you give thanks, the more you find things to be thankful for.

Shine your stars, work your horses, fix your problems and get rid of your dead wood.

The difference between cocky and confidence is that a cocky player always has an excuse.

I don't know the key to success, but the key to failure is trying to please everybody.

The best asset a coach can have is poor hearing.

A little negative thing must be dealt with immediately before it becomes a big negative thing.

The worst thing you can do for someone is to do something for them they can and should do for themselves.

A tough day at the office is even tougher when your OFFICE contains spectator seating.

People need to know what you stand for, AND what you won't stand for.

If you pay attention to the grandstands...it won't be long before you join them.

It is impossible to defeat an ignorant man in an argument.

A lot of people want to coach ball games, it's just that most don't have the balls to do it.

If a coach starts listening to fans, he winds up sitting next to them.

Never let other people's hang-ups about you restrict your life.

If you don't stand for something, you'll fall for anything.

I sought advice and cooperation from those around me—but not permission.
                                    Muhammad Ali

Don't find fault—find a remedy.

Can you play if you never play?

Fair is not always equal.

Don't allow your ego to be aligned too closely to your position.

The collapse of character begins with compromise.

Our lives begin to end the day we become silent about things that matter.
                    Martin Luther King, Jr.

Courage is what it takes to stand up and speak. Courage is also what it takes to sit down and listen.

Do what you feel in your heart to be right, for you'll be criticized anyway.

In order for somebody to pay attention to you, or his teammates, he has to feel confident about who he is.
                    Mike Krzyzewski

Don't free a camel of the burden of his hump; you may be freeing him from being a camel.

Sometimes it's worse to win a fight than to lose.

The trouble with most of us is that we would rather be ruined by praise than saved by criticism.

Of all our troubles, great and small, the greatest are those that don't happen at all.

They may forget what you said, but they will never forget how you made them feel.

If you don't make a total commitment to whatever you're doing, then you start looking to bail out the first time the boat starts leaking. It's tough enough getting that boat to shore with everybody rowing, let alone when a guy stands up and starts putting his jacket on.
                    Lou Holtz

Some people are born on third base and go through life thinking they hit a triple.

Coaches have to watch for what they don't want to see and listen to what they don't want to hear.

Never underestimate the power of stupid people in large groups.

Rule on meeting with parents. Talk about anything except playing time. You'll be surprised at how few meetings you'll have.

Being punished isn't enjoyable.
While it's happening it hurts.
But afterwards we can see the result.
A quiet growth in character and
grace.

Hebrews 12:11

Dissensions, like small streams, are first begun

Scarce seen they rise, but gather as they run

So lines that from their parallel decline

More they proceed the more they still disjoin.

There are six things the Lord hates, no, seven that are detestable to Him: haughty eyes, a lying tongue, hands that shed innocent blood, a heart that devises wicked schemes, feet that are quick to rush into evil, a false witness who pours out lies, and a man who stirs up dissension among brothers.

Proverbs 6:16-19

Hatred stirs up dissension, but love covers over all wrongs.

He that is master of himself, will soon be master of others.

He that brings good news knocks hard.

It takes just as little time to see the positive side of life as it does the negative side.

The masters all have the ability to discipline themselves to eliminate everything except what they are trying to accomplish.

Any fool can criticize, condemn, and complain—and most fools do.

Dale Carnegie

If we don't change the direction we're going, we're likely to end up where we're headed.

The old law about an 'eye for an eye' leaves everybody blind.

Martin Luther King, Jr.

Commitment to the team—there is no such thing as in-between, you are either in or out.

Pat Riley

Loyalty is very important when things get a little tough, as they often do when the challenge is great. Loyalty is a powerful force in producing one's individual best and more so in producing a team's best.

John Wooden

Teamwork is not a preference, it is a requirement.

Make sure team members know they are working with you, not for you.

Ask not what your teammates can do for you. Ask what you can do for your teammates.

When elephants fight, it's the grass that suffers.

Power is not revealed by striking hard or often, but by striking true.

When a team becomes infected, players who create 20 percent of the results will begin believing they deserve 80 percent of the rewards.

By union the smallest states thrive; by discord the greatest are destroyed.

To be trusted is a greater compliment than to be loved.

Jealousy—the jaundice of the soul.

A little rebellion now and then is a good thing.
                    Thomas Jefferson

I have always thought the actions of men to be the best interpreters of their thoughts.

Facts do not cease to be just because they are ignored.

He that will not apply new remedies must expect new evils.

A leader is either on top of events or if he hesitates, events will be on top of him.

Instead of loving your enemies, treat your friends a little better.

The critic is the one who knows the price of everything and the value of nothing.

The stones that critics hurl with harsh intent a man may use to build a monument.

If you succeed in life you must do it in spite of the efforts of others to pull you down. There is nothing in the idea that people are willing to help those who help themselves. People are willing to help a man who can't help himself but as soon as a man is able to help himself and does it, they join in making his life as uncomfortable as possible.

He who would acquire fame must not show himself afraid of censure. The dread of censure is the death of genius.

File Thirteen

The Postseason

The playoffs. A time to survive and advance. Lose and go home. It is easy for players and coaches to change as tension begins to build when the playoffs start. The important thing is to stay focused, confident and keep doing things that have made your season a success. Here are a few quotes to help prepare your team for the postseason.

I told them that if I laid a two-by-four across the room, everybody there could walk across it and not fall, because our focus would be that we were going to walk that two-by-four. But if I put that same two-by-four ten stories high between two buildings only a few would make it, because the focus would be on falling. Then I said, Your focus right now has to be as if we're playing on the practice field in front of nobody. If you let it overwhelm you that it'll be the most watched sporting event in the world, that there'll be 3000 media people here—if you make it bigger than life that will be a distraction. And that's the crux of this game. Focus on the two-by four.

> Jimmy Johnson
> preparing the
> Dallas Cowboys for
> the 1993 Super Bowl

As long as we have a chance to beat you—we'll take it.

It's absurd to increase one's luggage as one nears the journey's end.

Fortune favors the bold but abandons the timid.

Often times the roughest road may be the best way to where you want to go.

There is a very basic difference between an ordinary desire and a burning desire. A burning desire is a desire so strong that you believe yourself already in possession of its objective before you start to acquire it. It possesses your heart and soul completely. A burning desire will goad you to achievement.

Motivation is what gets you started. Habit is what keeps you going.

The person who is not afraid to fail seldom has to face it.

Championships are won by uncommon people because they are willing to do the things a common person won't do. A common person is basically lazy and frightful. Uncommon people are not afraid and the greater the challenge; the greater their determination becomes.

The ideal way to win a championship is step-by-step. You're always building.

Courage is fear holding a minute longer.

People who can't handle pressure sense that time speeds up. Things happen more quickly and they forget to do things. Those that handle pressure find that their sense of time slows down.

When two opponents of similar strength meet, often the determining factor is the desire and belief in oneself.

It is hard to separate the mental from the physical. So much of what you do physically happens because you thought about it and mentally prepared for it.

Playoff Theorem—Believe, Play Hard, Have Fun.

Focus on the process and not the product.

Anyone can be good only special people become great.

The playoffs are like a grindstone. Whether they grind you down or polish you up depends upon what you're made of.

The greatest efforts in sports came when the mind is as still as a glass lake.

Talent wins games, but teamwork and intelligence wins championships.

The object of war is not to die for your country, but make the other bastard die for his.
                    General Patton

Show me a guy who is afraid to look bad, and I'll show you a guy you can beat every time.

You have to expect things of yourself before you can do them.

You have no control over what the other guy does. You only have control over what you do.

There's no substitute for guts.

The best inspiration is not to outdo others, but to outdo ourselves.

He came, he saw, he conquered.

Carpe diem (Seize the day).

One falls to the ground in trying to sit on two stools.

Victory belongs to the most persevering.

Never give in. Never, Never, Never, Never!
                              Winston Churchill

At all times it is better to have a method.

The habit of persistence is the habit of victory.

How hard would you play today if there were no tomorrow?

Champions aren't made in the gyms. Champions are made from something they have deep inside them—a desire, a dream, a vision.

I firmly believe that any man's finest hour—his greatest fulfillment to all he holds dear—is that moment when he has worked his heart out in a good cause and lies exhausted on the field of battle, victorious.
                              Vince Lombardi

When I go out on the ice, I just think about my skating. I forget it is a competition.
                              Katarina Witt

Besides pride, loyalty, discipline, heart, and mind, confidence is the key to all the locks.
                              Joe Paterno

We must either find a way or make one.

Before you can win a game, you have to not lose it.

Play like you're in first, but train like you're in second.

The race isn't over until you cross the finish line. You'll be surprised at how much can change in the last twenty strides.

Passion, not pedigree, will win in the end.

Never underestimate the heart of a champion.

Rudy Tomjanovich

Being courageous requires no exceptional qualifications, no magic formula, no special combination of time, place and circumstance. It is an opportunity that sooner or later is presented to us all.

John F. Kennedy

Any time you try to win everything you must be willing to lose everything.

Anybody can be nobody, but it takes a man to be somebody.

Whenever two teams or players of equal ability play, the one with the greater courage will win.

I am the greatest. I said that even before I knew I was.

Muhammad Ali

To be a star and to stay a star; you've got to have certain air of arrogance about you, a cockiness, a swagger on the field that says, "I can do this and you can't stop me."

Joe Morgan

Dance with the one who brought you.

You can't tell someone to 'go for it' and be careful at the same time.

In our lives we will encounter many challenges, and tomorrow we face one together. How we accept the challenge and attack the challenge head on is only about us—no one can touch that. If we win or lose this weekend, it will not make a difference in our lives. But why we play and how we play will make a difference in our lives forever. When all is said and done, it's not the shots that won the championship that you remember, but the friendships you made along the way.

You can want it too much. You can try too hard. There comes a point where you have to let your muscle memory kick in.

Pressure is something you feel when you don't know what you're doing.

A true champion knows how to overcome doubts, manages doubts and learns how to turn them into motivation.

If you start thinking of pressure, it's because you start to think of failure.

Tommy Lasorda

You need your opponent to play. The player across from you wants to win as much as you do. You need him to test you and you need to test him. That's what competition is all about.

File Fourteen

Season's End

Finding the right words for the end of the season is often difficult. Whether you're feeling jubilation or dejection, saying the right thing after the journey has ended can have a powerful impact on the lives of your student-athletes. Encouraging them in other aspects of their lives can make a huge difference as some begin to prepare for life away from their sport.

There's a time for departure even if there is no certain place to go.

Success isn't how far you got, but the distance you traveled from where you started.

Success is a piece of mind which is a direct result of self-satisfaction in knowing you did your best to become the best that you are capable of becoming.

The reward of a thing well done is to have done it.

Wake up today and enjoy today. You have no control over tomorrow and you've lost yesterday. Go inning by inning.

Joe Torre

Success is a journey—not a destination.

It's good to have an end to journey toward but it's the journey that matters in the end.

Do not follow where the path may lead; go instead where there is no path and you leave a trail.

Happiness lies in the joy of achievement and the thrill of creative effort.

Success has always been easy to measure. It is the distance between one's origins and one's final achievement.

Somebody will always break your records. It is how you live that counts.

By your own soul learn to live, and if men thwart you, take no heed, if men hate you, have no care; sing your song, dream your dream, hope your hope and pray your prayer.

It's not the honor you take with you but the heritage you leave behind.

A champion in life is more important than a gold trophy. It stays with you forever.

The only thing on this earth that will never die...is a memory.

I have fought a good fight, I have finished my course. I have kept the faith.

II Timothy 4:7

A man is not old until regrets takes the place of dreams.

Always be Number one to yourself.

Experience is not what happens to a man; it is what a man does with what happens to him.

The journey is the reward.

I may not have gone where I intended to go, but I think I have ended up where I intended to be.

In the end, everything is a gag.

The greatest use of life is to spend it for something that will outlast it.

The doing is often more important than the outcome.

Continual improvement is an unending journey.

Be open to your dreams, people. Embrace that distant shore, because our mortal journey is over all too soon.

You've achieved success in your field when you don't know whether what you're doing is work or play.

Try not to become a man of success but rather to become a man of value.

A great secret of success is to go through life as a man who never gets used up.

Success is liking yourself, liking what you do, and liking how you do it.

He has achieved success who has lived well, laughed often, and loved much.

Success is accomplishing what you want. Happiness is enjoying it.

Tradition never graduates.

Don't cry because it's over—smile because it happened.

If

If you can keep your head when all about you
Are losing theirs and blaming it on you;
If you can trust yourself when all men doubt you,
But make allowance for their doubting too;
If you can wait and not be tired by waiting,
Or, being lied about, don't deal in lies,
Or, being hated, don't give way to hating,
And yet don't look too good, nor talk too wise;
If you can dream - and not make dreams your master;
If you can think - and not make thoughts your aim;
If you can meet with triumph and disaster
And treat those two imposters just the same;
If you can bear to hear the truth you've spoken
Twisted by knaves to make a trap for fools,
Or watch the things you gave your
life to broken,
And stoop and build 'em up with worn-out tools;
If you can make one heap of all your winnings
And risk it on one turn of pitch-and-toss,
And lose, and start again at your beginnings
And never breath a word about your loss;
If you can force your heart and nerve and sinew
To serve your turn long after they are gone,
And so hold on when there is nothing in you
Except the Will which says to them: "Hold on";
If you can talk with crowds and keep your virtue,
Or walk with kings - nor lose the common touch;
If neither foes nor loving friends can hurt you;
If all men count with you, but none too much;
If you can fill the unforgiving minute
With sixty seconds' worth of distance run,
Yours is the Earth and everything that's in it,
And - which is more - you'll be a Man my son!

Rudyard Kipling

Good luck to you and your team. May you
accomplish all of your goals each and every
season!

5610712R1

Made in the USA
Lexington, KY
28 May 2010